MORE
Liverpool
MEMORIES

The publishers would like to thank the following companies for their

support in the production of this book

Main Sponsor

Eli Lilly and Company Limited, Speke Operations

Arena Housing Association
Balfour Beatty
The Blue Coat School
Liverpool College
Andrew Collinge Hairdressing
Mersey Docks & Harbour Company
Getrag Ford Transmissions
Hayes & Finch
T J Hughes Ltd
Jacob's Bakery
Morris Jones & Son
Robert Lunt & Sons Ltd
Medicash Health Benefits Limited
Merchant Taylors' School
Merseytravel
Porter Bros Ltd
Royal & SunAlliance
Silverbeck Rymer
The Venmore Partnership
Yorkshire Copper Tube

First published in Great Britain by True North Books Limited
England HX3 6AE
01422 344344

ISBN 1 903204 88 7

Text, design and origination by True North Books Limited
Printed and bound by Charlesworth Press, Wakefield, UK

MORE *Liverpool* MEMORIES

CONTENTS

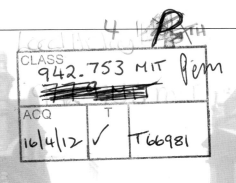

INTRODUCTION

Our city is, perhaps, the most vibrant one in the United Kingdom. Certainly, it has a wealth of history, culture, tradition and interest, allied to a unique personality that other places struggle to match. 'More Liverpool Memories' is the latest in a series of True North books that helps the reader capture a taste of the real city, its heart and soul coming alive thanks to a delightful selection of images and thought-provoking prose that accompanies them. This book takes a look at the city and earlier generations. Times and places change, but memories live on forever. Some are wrapped in joy, others enshrouded in grief, but they are nonetheless real and important to us. Perhaps some of things we recall are a little hazy in detail, so it is good to have photographs that pinpoint buildings and events just as they really were. They can help the past come flooding back to days when the dockland area meant shipyards and not restaurants and penthouses.

'More Liverpool Memories' transports us back to the age when men offered their seats on the bus to ladies who then smiled and actually said their thanks. Neighbours knew each other's names and their business, too. Children played in the street, safe in the knowledge that someone they knew and trusted was close by. They had seasons for marbles and conkers and there were special rhymes to be sung when playing two ball or hopscotch. Schools were places of education and not fortresses protected by security doors. Women were proud to be housewives, rather than apologising for relying on the man to provide the family income. They had marriages, not partnerships, and were able to keep in touch with their own mothers as they lived just round the corner. Holidays were taken at New Brighton, Blackpool and Rhyl when going abroad meant a week in Benllech Bay on Anglesey. Of course, the good old days were not as wonderful as old-timers would have you believe. There was the unemployment of the interwar depression years, the destruction and horror created by the second war with Germany and the austerity of the decade that followed. This book does not duck the sad times, but makes no apologies for celebrating those

that we remember with affection and pride. Liverpool has an important history of its own, stretching back some 2,000 years to the time when a settlement first appeared on the banks of the Mersey. This grew into a thriving fishing village during the Saxon era. However, it had not gained sufficient significance to be included in the 11th century Domesday Book. But, King John recognised the growing importance of the place known variously as 'Liuerpul' or 'Leuerepul' in 1207 when he granted it a charter that effectively founded the city that is our home today. The King wanted a port in the district that was free from the control of the Earl of Chester. People were encouraged to come and settle here with each one being given his own plot of land or 'burgage' for which he had to pay rent of 1s (5p) a year. The original settlement was situated on a sandstone ridge between the River Mersey and a tidal creek named The Pool. There are no traces of the medieval buildings left, but the layout of these streets has survived in the area around Castle Street, Dale Street, Tithebarn Street and Chapel Street. By 1235, a small castle had been built and Liverpool served as a dispatch point for troops sent to Ireland. A further charter, granted by Henry III, was an important landmark, as it remained the governing charter of the borough until 1626. It conceded that Liverpool should be a free borough for ever; thus securing the privileges already conferred by King John.

But, Liverpool remained relatively unimportant. In the middle of the 16th century the population of Liverpool was only around 500 and the port was regarded as a mere minor subsidiary of Chester until the 1650s. A number of battles for the town were waged during the English Civil War, including an 18 day siege in 1644, but Liverpool did not feature as a major player in British history until the developments in the 18th and 19th centuries. As trade from the West Indies was added to that of Ireland and Europe, Liverpool began to grow. The first wet dock in Britain was built in Liverpool in 1715. Substantial profits from the slave trade helped the town to prosper and rapidly grow and by 1750 there was a population of some 22,000. As the industrial revolution at home grew apace and Lancashire became one of the major centres of the textile trade, imports of cotton were largely transferred from London to Liverpool. The opening of the railway link with Manchester in 1830 and subsequent extensions helped the town increase in status as a trading centre. Eight new docks were built in the same period, culminating in Merseyside's pride and joy, the Albert Dock, in 1846. By the 1861 census, there were 440,000 inhabitants.

In the early 20th century, trade continued to boom and included the shipyards and engineering factories as major employers. Many of the fine buildings that we can see date from around the turn of that century. The most notable of these are, possibly, the Liver, Cunard and Port of Liverpool Buildings, along with the Anglican Cathedral. As an important maritime centre, the city suffered from considerable bomb damage during World War II and many attractive buildings were lost. Regeneration in the second half of the 20th century was slow to gather pace and the local economy declined as the docks and shipyards closed. By 1980 nearly a third of the workforce was unemployed. In more recent times, things have started to look up. The waterfront has been reborn and modern industry has taking a liking to the city. Liverpool will be the European Capital of Culture in 2008.

Although it is important to get a historical perspective when considering the contents of this book, 'More Liverpool Memories' is not a dry and dusty historical tome. It is a stroll down memory lane and an opportunity to relive those sights, sounds and activities that made the fairly recent past such an interesting part of our development. As you turn the pages listen out for the sound of Pete Best's drumming on a Beatles' track recorded on a bootleg tape in Hamburg, see if you can spot John Collier's 'window to watch' as you go shopping or try to recognise the squat lines of the Morris Cowley turning into Lime Street. Perhaps you might find the ghosts of Harry Catterick and Bill Shankly gazing across Stanley Perk from opposite sides, trying to outshine one another as the top soccer manager of his era. So get into the mood before you look at the first photograph or read the initial caption. Get out the Dansette, put a 45 on the turntable and let Billy Fury's 'Halfway to Paradise' take you all the way there. Remember when children bought two ounces of sherbet lemons and penny Arrow bars and cloth was sold by the yard, not the metre. Think back to the days when we saw men drink from glasses, not directly from the bottle, and women enjoyed a sweet sherry rather than a pint of lager. There was a time when grass was something that you mowed on a Sunday afternoon instead of smoking secretively and footballers with Brylcreemed hair played at centre forward and not as pony-tailed strikers. If you like to indulge in nostalgia, the rest is for you.

AT LEISURE

Now then, ducks, mind how you go. But, the ducks in question were not the youngsters anxious to have a ride on the sands at New Brighton, but the nickname given to these vehicles that was taken from the acronym applied to them. However, it is not a true one as DUKW, as the machine was called, was merely made up of a set of code letters. D meant the date of the year of first manufacture, namely 1942, U, for some reason, meant 'amphibian', K was for the drive to all wheels and W referred to dual axles. Whoever came up with these letters made a lucky choice because the approximate pronunciation as a single word made the vehicle memorable. The DUKW was the product of two very impressive parents. The General Motors Corporation provided the automotive components and the celebrated New York City yacht designers, Sparkman and Stephens, gave the new vehicle its sea-going capabilities. Strangely at first the US Army did not greet it with any enthusiasm, until fate intervened. It is now part of company legend that, when a US Coastguard ship was wrecked off Provincetown, Massachusetts, it was a DUKW that braved high seas and high winds to bring the seven man crew to safety. With publicity like that its future was secure. Seen here in 1946, the New Brighton Duck was one of many that rivalled the donkey in giving rides on British beaches.

Above: All too often, over the years many of Britain's seaside towns have lost the piers that used to adorn them. In the distance there is a little piece of history that was once the pride and joy of New Brighton. Its pier opened in September 1867, replacing one that was solely used for access to the ferry. The council took it over in 1928, extensively repairing and restoring it before its reopening in 1931. Some referred to the resort as being the Blackpool of Liverpool. New Brighton Tower, sadly destroyed by fire in 1969, the pier that went in the 1980s and the open air swimming pool, demolished in 1990, all belong to a yesteryear when we took our holidays much closer to home than the jet-setting folk of modern times. The miniature railway, chuffing along the promenade past the children's playground in those early postwar days, was just one of the delights that thrilled the kiddies. They rode on the swingboats, ran across the sands with shrimping nets and watched with a mixture of awe and amusement at the antics of Mr Punch, Judy, the policeman and strings of sausages. There was just enough time for a threepenny ride on the back of Ned the donkey before being whisked off to bed in a nearby guesthouse.

Theatre going is a pleasure for both young and old. Little ones learn to experience the magic of live performances when they attend their first pantomime. They can graduate through special children's shows, such as the ones when Sooty or Postman Pat comes to town, through to programmes of dance and music. By the time they are in their teens, youngsters are ready to take on board musicals, Shakespeare comedies and plays with a light-hearted content. Eventually they can graduate to meatier stuff, as this 1957 audience was doing. Changes in writing style were affecting the sort of drama that hit the boards and our bookshelves. The Noel Coward style of middle class 'so awfully, awfully sweet of you, Charles' sort of prose was becoming passé as the 'angry young men', such as John Braine, John Osborne and Alan Sillitoe, provided a more down to earth and grittier form of writing. Arthur Miller was an American of a similar genre in that his writing was fuelled by tough, personal experiences during the depression years. His play 'A View from the Bridge', directed by Sam Wanamaker (1919-93), was the attraction at the Shakespeare Theatre that first opened in 1888 on Fraser Street. Wanamaker was born in Chicago, but moved to Britain in 1949. As well as being a respected actor and director, he was the prime mover behind the Shakespeare Globe Trust in Southwark.

Below: Mum and dad chatted over their daughter's head about the good time they had enjoyed at Wilkie's Mammoth Circus. Does the little lass, now just about using her bus pass, recall the days out at New Brighton and the special treat she had that day? The ringmaster with the full moustache, cracking his whip, introduced a whole host of variety acts to the sawdust ring. Children looked on in awe as the lion tamer risked life and limb inside the cage with the big cats. Pretty girls in sequined leotards stood on the backs of horses that cantered around the big top and the animals tossed their plumed heads as if to illustrate their own sense of importance. Up aloft, the high wire walkers and trapeze artists raised the temperature with their death defying stunts, while down below sealions played motor horns and tossed footballs into the air with their snouts. Then it was time for the clowns. Their garishly painted faces, funny hair and outlandish clothes made the kiddies laugh hysterically, particularly when they fell over their big feet and drowned the ringmaster with buckets of water. Occasionally, we would also see parades of elephants and camels, but the magic of the circus was in the speciality acts and the antics of the clowns. 'Can we come back tomorrow, Dad? Please'.

Below: The chair lift above New Brighton's funfair gave a panoramic view of the stalls and sideshows below, though it was not a place for anyone with a touch of vertigo. Modern health and safety officials would turn apopleptic at the buckets and flimsy guard rails, but who needed namby-pamby regulations when we had seen off all that Hitler could throw at us a decade earlier? Down below the passengers' feet, people tried to hook ducks to win a small prize. Those dratted birds always wobbled just as you were about to get one. When success was achieved what did it matter that the threepence you had paid for a go only yielded a prize worth half that? The same was true on the dart stall where 'arrers' with doctored flights could not travel in a straight line and stick into three separate playing cards, even if Eric Bristow's dad was chucking them. The coconuts were glued on, the rifle sights lopsided and the Wild Man from Borneo was really Alf Higgins from Tranmere, but we did not care. We enjoyed ourselves in the good old British way, accepting the tricks of the trade as part of the fun of the fair. Still, Tiddles was happy when we brought home a goldfish in a plastic bag. She purred away to her heart's content waiting for everyone to go to bed.

Above: All the fun of the fair was to be had at New Brighton. The Tower Grounds opened in the summer of 1897 and soon became a magnet for those on Merseyside who wanted a fun packed day out. There was so much to capture the imagination and to thrill and entertain both young and old alike. Young lovers cuddled together on the ghost train, with the girl screaming in mock terror as a silly looking skeleton appeared or a mock cobweb brushed her face. Swing boats whizzed backwards and forwards and those with a strong stomach took to the air on the Big Wheel. Greasy haired lads jumped from car to car on the dodgems, collecting the tanners from the drivers who indulged in fantasies about being American stock car drivers as they aimed their vehicles at each other. Sparks flew from the connecting rods above them and the smell of burning rubber hung in the air. Elsewhere, riders on the waltzers enjoyed having their necks jerked back as some form of centrifugal force took hold and the cars lurched this way and that. Younger funseekers enjoyed more sedate roundabouts, sitting in toy fire engines where they could fight over whose turn it was to ring the bell. The older generation just liked being there, thinking back to when they were young as they risked their dentures on a toffee apple.

There were other funfairs and playgrounds in New Brighton that complemented the much larger Tower Grounds. Here, close to the promenade, a special set of rides was designed for the kiddies. The 1948 mini version of the big wheel, though nobody had thought to use the word that Alec Issigonis and Mary Quant would later make famous with his car and her skirt, was just right for little ones. Not too high, but it could still give small children an element of the thrill experienced by their big brothers and sisters on the real thing. The merry-go-round, turned at a modest pace. Nippers rode aboard exotic animals that included llamas, zebras, giraffes and camels and waved to doting grandparents as they went past them. Most of the children seen here will have grandchildren of their own by now and will regale them with stories of what is was like having fun without the need to insert a DVD into a machine or switch on a computer. In those early postwar years, adults were only too happy to see that their children could enjoy themselves without the need to keep an ear open for the air raid siren. They could relax for the first time in years and what better place to do it than at the seaside?

EVENTS OF THE 1950s

WHAT'S ON?

Television hit Britain in a big way during the 1950s. Older readers will surely remember 'Double Your Money, Dixon of Dock Green and 'Dragnet' (whose characters' names were changed 'to protect the innocent').
Commercial television was introduced on 22nd September 1955, and Gibbs SR toothpaste were drawn out of the hat to become the first advert to be shown. Many believed adverts to be vulgar, however, and audiences were far less than had been hoped for.

GETTING AROUND

The year 1959 saw the development of the world's first practical air-cushion vehicle - better known to us as the hovercraft. The earliest model was only able to travel at slow speeds over very calm water and was unable to carry more than three passengers. The faster and smoother alternative to the sea ferry quickly caught on, and by the 1970s a 170-ton car-carrying hovercraft service had been introduced across the English Channel.

SPORTING CHANCE

The four-minute mile had remained the record since 1945, and had become regarded as virtually unbreakable. On 6th May 1954, however, Oxford University student Roger Bannister literally ran away with the record, accomplishing the seemingly impossible in three minutes 59.4 seconds. Bannister collapsed at the end of his last amazing lap, even temporarily losing his vision. By the end of the day, however, he had recovered sufficiently to celebrate his achievement in a London night club!

DOWN AT THE DOCKS

The floating landing stage at Prince's Dock stretched for about half a mile and had its rail link behind at Riverside Station that gave almost direct access to the mighty ocean-going liners that graced the Mersey estuary. Just watching the way in which passengers, luggage and mountains of provisions were taken aboard was a spectacle in its own right and a credit to the organisational skills of those in charge. In 1951, the country was getting back on its feet after the privations of the 1939-45 war. We had not turned the corner completely, as it would not be until the late 1950s that we entered the 'never had it so good' years, but we were on the way. As a gesture of faith in a better future, the government sponsored the Festival of Britain so that, as Herbert Morrison put it, 'people can give themselves a pat on the back'. The intention was to provide a spectacle of fun, fantasy and colour that would be in complete contrast to the grim pillboxes and utilitarian Nissen huts of wartime. Pragmatists on Merseyside viewed it as more of a London thing and a sop to the general public by deflecting attention away from the rationing that was still there in part. At least we could boast that we had sporting champions as boxer Randolph Turpin beat Sugar Ray Robinson, Max Faulkner won the Open golf championship and athlete MacDonald Bailey set a record for the 100 metres.

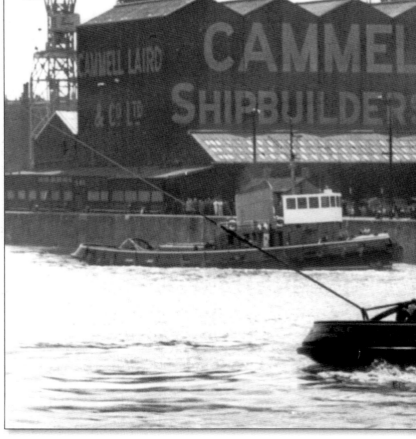

Above: The river was Liverpool's lifeblood. The original creek that provided the sheltered place from where troops could be sent to Ireland in the early 13th century is now somewhere under the Pier Head, but the port and river traffic grew significantly to become the major force in the economy in the years that followed. By the middle of the 18th century, partly because of problems with our French and Spanish enemies making life difficult for shipping in the Channel and off the Bay of Biscay, Liverpool became the favoured port for many merchants. It was a safer embarkation point than London for the growing trade with America and the West Indies. It was important that the estuary should be kept operational at all times and represent safe passage for all the vessels coming to use it. The huge rise in shipping entering our waters in the 19th and early 20th centuries made this even more important. Lightships, such as the 'Morecambe Bay', acted as markers where reefs and sandbanks threatened the cargo and passenger ships. They also shone powerful beams and sounded warning horns when fog rolled in. In more recent times, large buoys, many of which gain their energy source from solar power, have replaced most of the ships.

The mighty cranes at the Cammell Laird yard dominate the skyline in this photograph from c1960. The famous shipyard in Birkenhead, opposite Liverpool on the River Mersey, built hundreds of ships from the 1830s onwards. Steam powered ferry boats were introduced on the river in the late 18th century and they helped open up the Wirral as a desirable spot from where wealthy merchants and businessmen could commute to an overcrowded Liverpool. It was only a short step from there to establishing companies on this side of the river. John Laird was one of those who seized his opportunity and, in 1824, built a boiler and ironworks in Birkenhead. This was the embryo of what would become the internationally famous Cammell Laird shipyard. It was also responsible for many innovations and records in its field. These included the first screw driven ship, the 'Robert F Stockton' in 1838, the first iron ship to sail round the Cape of Good Hope, the 'Nemesis' in 1840 and the first ship to be fitted with watertight bulkheads, the 'Lady Lansdowne', built in 1830. These partitions could be sealed to prevent flooding or fire spreading throughout the ship. In this picture we can see the bows of the 'Windsor Castle', a passenger and cargo ship. She was launched by Elizabeth, the Queen Mother in 1959. The ship was primarily intended to serve on the Royal Mail route to South Africa and boasted the largest shaft horsepower ever built into a merchant ship.

EVENTS & OCCASIONS

Below: Waiting for the Isle of Man steam packet tried everybody's patience. We think we have it badly these days, having to check in at John Lennon Airport two or three hours before a continental flight, but at least there are bars, shops and comfy seats to help while away the time. In 1948, there were some wooden chairs and that was about it. The crossing to Douglas was a popular one at holiday time and was about as far as our continental horizons and wage packets stretched. Hotels and guest houses all across the island and down to Port St Mary and Port Erin were full to bursting every summer. Many families went to the same one, year in year out and booked for the following summer on the final morning of the current holiday. In the lower centre of the photograph, three women were in earnest conversation. Probably, Ena, Martha and Minnie, the trio of ladies who used to inhabit the Rovers' Return snug on 'Coronation Street', were based on such as these. The one on the right has something of Hilda Ogden, now that we look more closely, but it does not take too much imagination to put words into their mouths. 'Did you see the state of Mrs Wood's front doorstep this morning? I don't know what she cleans it with but it looks more donkey than stone.' 'And to think she's got net curtains an' all.'

Here today, gone tomorrow. He won't last. No one will remember him in two years' time. These are the sorts of phrases that those of us who are members of the wrinkly brigade happily trot out when discussing the pop stars of today. Of course, when we were teenagers there were proper artists whose work has stood the test of time. Cliff Richard still packs them in, Tommy Steele fills theatres and Elvis Presley's songs are played daily. And, let us not forget Mitchell Torok. Pardon, grandpa; who? We must admit that even pop quiz experts will be hard pushed to identify that particular act. Yet, despite his current obscurity, this 28 year old Texan had them queuing the length of

Dale Street in 1957. He was the special guest star who was to preside at the official opening of the Top Hat Record Bar. Pop music fans eagerly got him to autograph copies of his 78 vinyl pressing 'When Mexico gave up the rhumba', a quaint but successful attempt to cash in on the new rock and roll craze. It soared into the top 10 and he toured Britain on the strength of it, as a supporting act to Johnny Ray. Mitchell Torok began his career as a songwriter for various artists. His first hit, 'Mexican Joe', was a 1953 country smash for Jim Reeves and Torok had his own success as a singer with 'Caribbean', a top seller in America. He had one further small hit in Britain but continued to do well in his homeland as a composer.

Above: This picture shows a group of people who are mainly pensioners. It really is true, because that is where we are today. For those of us with grey hairs, thinning locks and expanding waistlines it might be difficult to convince our grandchildren that we were once like them. They tend to think that grandpa was born old! Well put them right and get them to look at this photograph of the English Electric children's party. Apart from the hairstyles and clothing, when boys and girls could be identified by what they wore, there is little that has changed in feeding youngsters at party time. Just provide cake, pop and a few sausage rolls and it is fiesta time. This was Christmas time in 1951 and the English Electric Company had taken it upon itself to act as a philanthropist. Not everybody could say the same, but this was one organisation that took its place in the general scheme of things with an eye to helping the needy as well as making a profit. These were orphaned kiddies who had been dealt a rough deal, partly by society, but mainly by circumstance. Quite a number could blame the war for the loss of their parents and it was good to see that there were people doing their best to help those less fortunate than themselves. Thanks to the Beatles' song, 'Strawberry Fields', most people will be familiar with the children's home in Woolton, run by the Salvation Army.

Below: It was always a proud day when a new ship was launched down the slipway. Anyone who had played a part in the creation of another vessel to leave the yard turned up for the official ceremony. Some risked life and limb getting the best vantage point and there was almost as much excitement as that generated by any Everton-Liverpool local derby, with the exception being that all of those in this crowd supported the same team. Cammell Laird of Birkenhead was the outfit that inspired the spectators on 18 July 1958. At the very same time as this, Prince Philip, the Duke of Edinburgh, was opening the Empire Games at Cardiff. That was of secondary importance in the shipyard as the gathered assembly was about to witness a rather special launching. Normally, there were fine words, a prayer or two and the smashing of a ceremonial champagne bottle. This day was slightly different. 'Talwar' was a frigate commissioned by the Indian Navy and the proceedings differed slightly from the norm. There were still the uplifting speeches but, when Mrs D Trivedi, the wife of the counsellor to the Indian High Commission, stepped forward prayers were said to Varuna, the Hindu god of the ocean. Good luck powder was applied to the ship, a garland of flowers hung on the prow and a decorated coconut broken on the bows.

Left: The English Electric Flower Show of 1954 attracted large numbers wanting to look at the attractive posies, bouquets, displays and floral arrangements. But, there were other centres of interest that siphoned off sections of the crowds and none more so than the area where Hornby had its exhibition. Never mind mother nature and all that blossomed elsewhere, here was a 'blooming' good way to spend an hour or so. Dads, a few mums and lots of children peered with fascination as the transformers were wired up to the track and Dublo locomotives whizzed through papier-mache tunnels and past bushes made from bits of foam that had been painted green. There were Dinky cars and figures of porters by the stations and you could lose yourself in another world at this part of the show. Clockwork motors powered the first Hornby trains produced in 1920, but a range that ran on mains electricity was introduced in 1925. However, by 1929 Hornby had evolved a much safer system and electric models worked from a six volt DC source that most of us remember. In 1938, Hornby Dublo ('00') was launched. This was approximately half the size of the 'o' gauge system the company originally used, except that the locomotives had cast metal bodies, not pressed metal, and the buildings were made of wood.

Below: Bluecoat Chambers, now an arts centre, was a well known charitable boarding school, founded in 1718. This was part of a 1960 exhibition mounted by the Cammell Laird engineering and shipbuilding company. Merseysiders were well used to seeing the huge cranes towering above the dockland, but even the most familiar young Scouser was impressed with this giant working model, made from Meccano. Every little lad has, at some time, received a visit from Father Christmas bearing one of these kits in his sack. The more enlightened parents made sure that the visitor from Lapland had a similar present for their daughter as well. When Frank Hornby applied for a patent in 1901 to protect an invention he called 'Improvements in Toy or Educational Devices for Children and Young People', nobody then could have imagined how this product would influence the modelling hobby that we know today. He soon put the invention into production under the name 'Mechanics Made Easy'. This led to the establishment of Meccano Ltd in 1907. The company was such a runaway success that Frank had to move his factory several times to new and larger premises. Meccano was to become one of the classic toys of all time. Following the acquisition in 1964 of Meccano Ltd by Lines Brothers, the parent company of Tri-ang Railways, the companies were merged the following year to become Tri-ang Hornby.

Below: The Woodside Ferry at Birkenhead provided one of the crossing points across the River Mersey. It linked to the railway system, providing a good service for commuters flocking to and fro across the water. The station replaced the one at Monks Ferry when it opened on 1 April 1878 as the terminus of the Chester to Birkenhead line that saw its first trains on 23 September 1840. The Chester and Birkenhead Company amalgamated with Birkenhead, Lancashire and Cheshire Railways in 1847. Woodside was one of a special breed of stations as it serviced trains, trams and ships alike. It closed on 6 November 1967 and became a car park. It was just one of ten such places from where travellers could embark across the river in Victorian times. How busy those links between the Wirral and Liverpool must have been as the Mersey was crossed and recrossed by scores of boats packed to the gunwales with passengers. By the 1920s some 32 million people were carried each year on the 10 minute journey, a staggering statistic that reinforces the importance of the ferry service to the daily life of so many. Gerry and the Pacemakers immortalised the service with their 1964 hit 'Ferry across the Mersey'. Here we see Woodside in 1953, proclaiming its support for Queen Elizabeth II's coronation celebrations.

During the second world war and the subsequent few years afterwards the city was well used to parades through the centre. What had been a show of strength and unity became a celebration for a job well done. As well as displays by the armed forces we also became used to seeing marches in honour of civic occasions and local dignitaries would don their chains of office as well as war medals and enjoy strutting their stuff. Normally, large crowds would accompany the parade, but on this occasion it seems as if Liverpuddlians had become blasé about the importance of such processions as only small knots of the general public stood on the pavements. The band appears to be a Salvation Army group, to judge from the uniforms of the men and women at the head of the crocodile. It headed across St George's Plateau in 1949, in front of St George's Hall outside which we can see the handsome standard lamps, entwined with dolphins, that line the walkway above the war memorial and the figures of Queen Victoria and Prince Albert, mounted on horseback. The area was cleared in the 1830s and work on the Hall began in 1842. At this time, Her Majesty was only five years into her reign. She acceded to throne at the tender age of 18 and the statue shows Victoria as she was at the time. For those of us more used to her as an elderly person in widow's weeds, it comes as a surprise to see a youthful, athletic woman.

Below: Legs and Co was a dance troupe on 'Top of the Pops' in the late 1970s. Perhaps this bevy of beauty, seen in the summer of 1953, inspired Flick Colby and her girls in later years. They certainly raised the temperature on the male population's brows. How could any red-blooded man fail to avoid a lingering look at this quartet of crackers? Advertising the toffee that gave Everton soccer club its nickname, these pretty milkmaids stood on the 'Toffee Maid' float that was part of the carnival put on to celebrate Coronation

Day on 2 June. In keeping with the rest of the country, Liverpool pushed the boat out in arranging festivities to mark the accession of Queen Elizabeth II. Down in London, the state coach carried the young monarch to Westminster Abbey in a scene described in reverential tones by that ace broadcaster, Richard Dimbleby. Television cameras relayed the proceedings to the limited number of homes that had the little, flickering black and white sets. Neighbours crowded into the front lounge of anyone lucky enough to have such a luxury. The nation was united behind the new queen and partied in a way that had not been seen since the celebrations that marked the end of the war, nearly eight years earlier.

Below: Rather unfortunately, behind this group of beauty queens posing on the fairground roundabout we can just make out a sign advertising the Chamber of Horrors! Let us hasten to add that our set of lovely ladies had absolutely no connection with that particular sideshow at the New Brighton pleasure grounds. The attraction of these pretty young things was apparent for all to see. As we can tell from their sashes, they represented various towns and cities in the northwest and were a prime example of fresh faced, young womanhood. In 1947 a beauty contest was part of the fun of the fair or a normal seaside event. Always conducted in a demure manner, even when parading in bathing costumes, these were ordinary mill girls, receptionists, typists and nurses who competed mainly for fun. They were a far cry from the gyrating girls who are employed in sordid bars in this day and age. The popularity of the humble beauty contest inspired Eric Morley to take matters further. The Mecca dancehalls organisation, of which he was a senior official, used to have fashion competitions and, in 1951 to tie in with the Festival of Britain, he launched the first Miss World contest. The simple beauty contest was soon big business and drew huge TV audiences in the 1970s before political correctness and the feminist lobby started to have an impact.

TRANSPORT

There is no chance of dumping your car in the middle of Lime Street these days. Well, you can leave it, but it will be towed away without ceremony in a trice. Short stay, regulated street parking and multi storey parks, such as the one at nearby Queen Square, are now the order of the day. It was a much less frenetic scene in c1950 as we looked across from the latter towards St George's Hall and the Wellington Column towards the left. Work on the hall, unique in terms of its architecture, function and history, began in 1842 to a design by Harvey Lonsdale Elmes. It opened in 1854 and represents the prosperity in Liverpool in the 19th century. With its splendid chandeliers and gilded plasterwork, it is one of the best assembly halls in Britain. The magnificent main hall is floored with Minton tiles and is 169 feet in length. The grand building on the opposite side of Lime Street is now part of the John Moores University. Originally the North Western Hotel, it was built in 1867 to the designs of Alfred Waterhouse. It served as the major hotel serving Lime Street, then a major terminus in the days of steam. This Grade II Listed building was revitalised and refurbished in the mid 1990s to incorporate the needs of students and consists of 246 study bedrooms in 60 flats of various sizes.

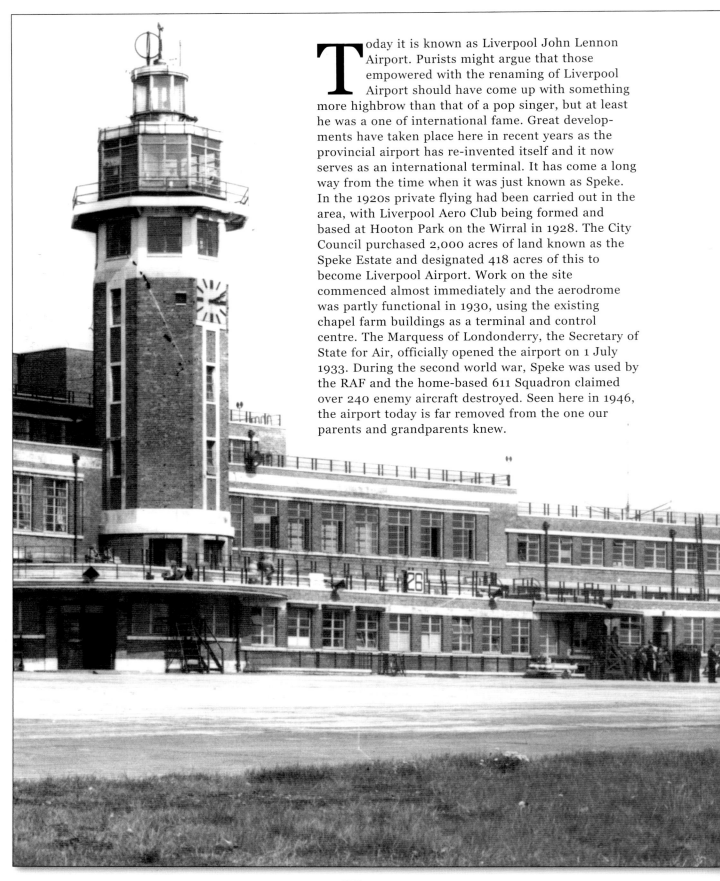

Today it is known as Liverpool John Lennon Airport. Purists might argue that those empowered with the renaming of Liverpool Airport should have come up with something more highbrow than that of a pop singer, but at least he was a one of international fame. Great developments have taken place here in recent years as the provincial airport has re-invented itself and it now serves as an international terminal. It has come a long way from the time when it was just known as Speke. In the 1920s private flying had been carried out in the area, with Liverpool Aero Club being formed and based at Hooton Park on the Wirral in 1928. The City Council purchased 2,000 acres of land known as the Speke Estate and designated 418 acres of this to become Liverpool Airport. Work on the site commenced almost immediately and the aerodrome was partly functional in 1930, using the existing chapel farm buildings as a terminal and control centre. The Marquess of Londonderry, the Secretary of State for Air, officially opened the airport on 1 July 1933. During the second world war, Speke was used by the RAF and the home-based 611 Squadron claimed over 240 enemy aircraft destroyed. Seen here in 1946, the airport today is far removed from the one our parents and grandparents knew.

Above: The prices sound as old fashioned as the vehicles at Geneva Motors, Renshaw Street. Who ever uses guineas these days? Younger readers might not even know what this figure meant. For the uninitiated, it was worth £1 1s or £1.05 in today's lingo. It was an odd amount, even to those of us used to calculating in pounds, shillings and pence. It was even worse when people expressed prices in half guineas or 10 s 6d (52.5p). The little Heinkel three wheeler 'bubble' car is a museum piece. Every generation seems to throw up an oddity. Remember Clive Sinclair's C5? The motor scooters were popular in 1960 and have continued to have their aficionados over the subsequent years. In the swinging 60s they became the symbol of all that was modern, hence the term 'mod' applied to their young riders. They were the sworn enemies of the 'rockers' who roared around on high powered bikes and loved Gene Vincent, Eddie Cochran and Johnny Kidd songs. They regarded the scooter riders on puny Lambretta or Vespa 150cc machines as somewhat effete, though they probably used words stronger than that to describe them. Mods liked the music of the Small Faces and other groups with long, shiny hair. Bank Holiday Mondays were often marred by pitched battles between the rival groups as they fought along the seafronts of our resorts

Above: Queensway, the Mersey Tunnel, operated maximum and minimum speed limits, as can be seen from this 1956 photograph. In the slow lane, 6 mph was the minimum and 21 mph the maximum. Switch to the fast lane and vehicles were expected to go at 21 to 30 mph. The person who thought up these figures must have had some reason for the arbitrary nature of the slowest speeds. It may be half a century ago, but which of these vehicles had to be regulated in order to ensure a rate of no less than that achieved by a pensioner on a pushbike? The styles of the vans and cars may have changed, but it is obvious that the congested nature of the tunnel is no new experience. The van on the right belonged to the Bedford based company, Cryselco. It was established in 1895 to manufacture the then new concept of electric lamps just 15 years after Thomas Edison had invented the light bulb. The name is a corruption of the original trading style of the Crystal Electric Company. The van alongside carried boxes of St Bruno, one of the most popular pipe tobaccos ever manufactured. Thomas Ogden first marketed St Bruno in 1896. Over 30 years earlier, in 1860, he opened the first of many tobacconists' shops in Park Lane, Liverpool. There are several Brunos who have been canonised, the most notable being an 11th century Benedictine from Cologne.

Right: There was once a time when the postman always rang twice. That was in real life and not just in a James Cain novel or Hollywood movies. As well as two deliveries a day, he even collected from village pillar boxes more than once and, should we ever forget, ran a Sunday collection as well. To think that automation, postcodes and efficient practices have reduced the service provided to the general public, rather than increase it, takes some understanding. It would not be too bad if all our correspondence got there the following day as it used to or that packages made it to their destinations in one piece. What price progress? Are we being too fanciful to think that, in 1958 we had a good deal from the GPO? These vans were part of the service we felt we could rely on. Pictured at Whitechapel Post Office, they were in the setted yard on which the new post office was later built. Town or city centre offices may soon be the only places where you can get your stamps and pension or have the Giro cheque cashed. Sub-post offices are fast becoming a thing of the past as village communities are denied the convenience of their own establishment. It might not be too long before small towns suffer the same fate. This is called 'rationalisation'.

Below: The rail link between Riverside Station and Pier Head at Prince's Dock opened in 1895, primarily for those wishing to meet or embark on a liner sailing the Atlantic. Some would use the facility as a means of starting a holiday away from these shores, but for many others it was the start of a new life in the land of Uncle Sam. It was also the point of both arrival and departure for troops during the second world war. The males in this photograph, seen well over half a century ago, illustrate the way that sartorial fashion was viewed at the time. Whatever the age group, there is a distinct similarity in the choice of clothing. Nearly all of them are wearing hats of one style or another and, without exception, are attired in suit, collar and tie. Lads were just miniature dads in those days. The youth on the right is, perhaps, the only one trying to show a little bit of individuality. His gaudy tie does mark him out as being someone who has a statement to make. It is reminiscent of the style favoured by that cheeky chappie, the comedian Max Miller, or by the sort of person grannie called a 'spiv'. His bareheaded counterpart to the right, though, looks certain to become something in the city as he gives the impression that he is a more earnest sort of soul.

Above: Looking out across the railway goods yards and the docks, this photograph was taken at Bankhall in Kirkdale in the early 1960s. The 'You're never alone with a Strand' is one of the most famous slogans from that era. First used in 1959, an imaginative campaign showed Frank Sinatra look-alike Terence Brooks lighting up on a lonely street corner. The accompanying caption reassured viewers that the cigarette provided great company as Cliff Adams' haunting instrumental played in the background. The ads were certainly popular and Adams' revamping of the 'Lonely Man Theme' later became a huge hit, but the unfortunate outcome was that consumers, subconsciously associating Strand with loneliness and unsociability, stayed away from the brand in their droves. It soon disappeared from the market and one of the biggest misfires of television advertising became a cult memory rather than a financial success. The other main advert on the hoardings had much more success. 'Drinka pinta milka day' was one of the most influential campaigns of the 1950s. The Milk Marketing Board followed it up in the early 1980s with 'Milk's gotta lotta bottle' as the same product claimed two high ranking places in TV's top 100 jingles. Some famous names have contributed to the writing of famous slogans. Among the most surprising are Salman Rushdie and Murray Walker. Respectively, they wrote 'naughty but nice' for cream cakes and 'a Mars a day helps you work, rest and play'.

Below: The Americans left these shores in 1945 with our thanks ringing in their ears for the job they had done in helping the war against the Nazis. The great friendship between the two nations was born out of adversity and continued to develop in peacetime. Under the lend-lease scheme begun before the USA entered the war, ammunition, tanks, airplanes and trucks, along with food and other raw materials, were loaned to Britain. These would be paid for eventually in kind or by indirect benefit. A further tranche of assistance for Europe was provided by the late 1940s' Marshall Plan that gave cash to economically damaged countries to help create stable conditions in which democratic institutions could survive. America feared the effect of communism. This consignment of Leyland buses was not, though, part of our payback scheme; it was an effort to sell this country to potential tourists and ensure that this country was on every American's itinerary when undertaking the grand tour. Our capital city had a London Bus Week in 1952 and these red doubledeckers, as described by Flanders and Swann in one of their songs, made their way across the big pond emblazoned with greetings and adverts. We knew that the Yanks were suckers for bits of quaint English customs and this form of transport might just inspire some to come over and sample our culture and traditions at first hand.

Regeneration after the second world war took a long time to complete. For years, bombsites were littered across the city, some still with lumps of concrete, bricks and rubble in their midst. At least they provided car parking space for office workers and shoppers coming into Liverpool. The cranes dominated the skyline throughout the 1950s as building work continued, seemingly at a non stop rate. In 1955 there was still much to do before the shopping heartland could be restored. It would be some time before the buildings at the junction of Lord Street and South Castle Street could be brought to life. In the distance, top right,

the Anglican Cathedral is the main feature that can be made out. In 1880, John Charles Ryle was appointed the first Bishop of Liverpool and was installed in Saint Peter's Church, a building described by the Rector of Liverpool as 'ugly & hideous'. In June 1901, at a meeting in the Town Hall, the decision was taken to build a worthy cathedral for the prosperous city of Liverpool. Giles Gilbert Scott and George Bodley were commissioned as the architects and King Edward VII laid the foundation stone in 1904. In June 1910, Bishop Chavasse and Cosmo Long, Archbishop of York and a future Archbishop of Canterbury dedicated the cathedral.

Eli Lilly - The answer that matters

One of this region's most important and respected enterprises is Eli Lilly and Company Ltd's bulk manufacturing facility based in Fleming Road, Speke. Both the company and plant have a remarkable history. Not only has the health of the local economy benefited enormously from the presence of the plant, but those who have worked there can also look back with pride at being involved in an enterprise which has made a vast contribution to the well-being of millions around the world.

Lilly began its UK operations in 1934 when it established a small sales office in central London. The company opened its first manufacturing facility outside the US in Basingstoke in 1939, the day after war was declared.

However, the story of Eli Lilly and Company goes back to 1876 when Company Founder Eli Lilly himself opened a small pharmaceutical business in Indianapolis in the USA.

At the age of 38 Colonel Eli Lilly had not had a happy life so far: he had been captured and become a prisoner during the American Civil War. During his captivity his wife had died in childbirth. On release from prison camp Eli tried his hand at being a cotton planter but went bankrupt. He put the last of his savings into another type of business entirely.

Seldom has $1,400 been better invested. Eli began with two employees and a month later would take on a third - his fourteen year old son, and eventual successor, Josiah Kirby Lilly.

Eli Lilly and Company was unorthodox from the start – its purpose was to specialise in "ethical" drugs to be dispensed at the suggestion of enlightened physicians, not at the eloquence of sideshow hucksters – the latter was a practice very common of the day. Colonel Eli had vowed that Lilly pharmaceuticals would be based on the best science of the day and quality was paramount. Eli Lilly famously said to his son, "take what you find here and make it better and better. No business worthwhile can be built upon anything but the best in everything" and the ethic continues to this day.

In the first year of business sales averaged less than $1,000 a month. A century later Eli Lilly and Company

Top left: Colonel Eli Lilly. *Below left:* Josiah K Lilly Sr, son of the founder. *Below:* Where it all began, Eli Lilly's small pharmaceutical company in Indianapolis, USA.

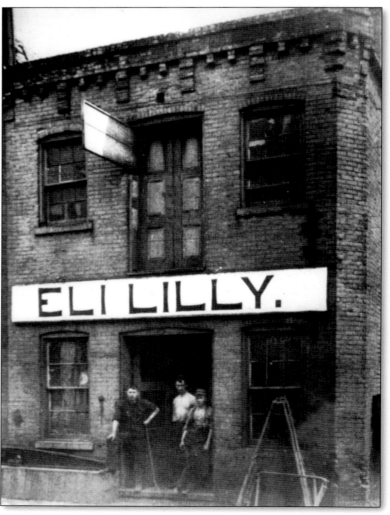

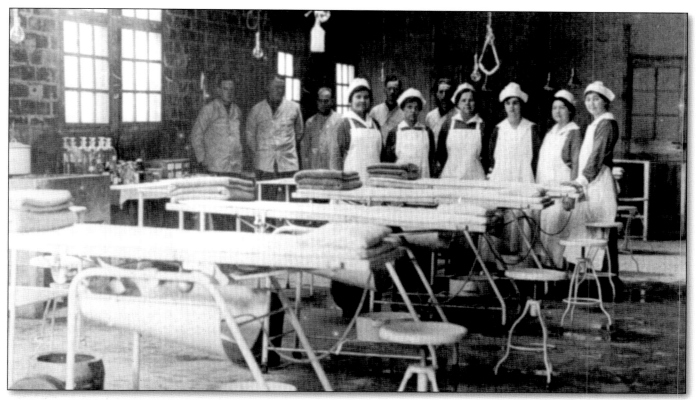

the greatest breakthroughs in modern medicine - they discovered insulin, the first substance found to help control diabetes. In May 1922 Eli Lilly staff were invited by the University of Toronto to help in developing a process for refining insulin and its manufacture. By August Lilly scientists had worked out improved methods for the purification and large-scale production of standardised insulin. Thanks to the work of Lilly by the end of 1923 insulin would become available to millions.

Meanwhile over on the other side of the Atlantic in Britain another important story was unfolding.

One of the most famous names in history is that of Alexander Fleming (1881-1955) and his discovery of penicillin in 1928.

would have more than 23,000 employees and annual sales worldwide of more than a billion dollars. Such growth however, must have been far from the mind of the young entrepreneur who set up in business in 1876.

The firm grew steadily and by 1898, when 'Colonel Eli' died, the firm was selling over 2,000 products, helping improve people's lives in areas where effective treatments had previously not been available.

It was to be insulin however, which propelled the company to the very forefront of the pharmaceutical industry. In 1921 Frederick G Banting and Charles H Best made one of

Every schoolchild can recall the tale of how in August 1928 Fleming was in his laboratory and about to wash out an old petri dish on which he had been cultivating some staphylococcus bacteria. Suddenly he noticed that a strange mould which had begun growing in the bottom of the dish was killing the bacteria.

*Top: A medical field hospital in Contrexeville, France, set up in 1917 during the first world war by Lilly in partnership with the American Red Cross. **Above left:** Lilly was among the first pharmaceutical companies to mass-produce penicillin.*

The mould turned out to be penicillin; Fleming's chance observation would lead to fame, fortune and a knighthood - and save the lives of millions.

Fleming gave us a new word 'penicillin' which he coined in a paper published in 1929 where he used the word as shorthand for the 'mould broth filtrate' which he had extracted from the penicillium whilst trying to distil the active ingredient in the mould.

But intriguingly Fleming completely failed to achieve anything useful with his interesting discovery. He did find that the extract 'penicillin' would attack a range of bacteria, but initially concluded that it was quite useless for treating the sick. The glory of the penicillin story passed to two other men: Howard Florey and Ernst Chain.

An Australian, Howard Walter Florey (1898-1968), was a Professor of Pathology in Oxford. In the mid-1930s Florey invited a German Jewish colleague anxious to quit Hitler's Germany, biochemist Ernst Boris Chain (1906-1979), to join his research team.

In the late 1930s Florey and Chain picked up the ball, which had been dropped by Fleming almost a decade earlier. Together the pair devised improved techniques for manufacturing and purifying penicillin before embarking on an extensive series of trials and experiments testing the substance's clinical efficacy against a variety of bacteria.

In 1940, following clinical tests on mice, the first human recipient of penicillin was an Oxford policeman with blood poisoning; he began to recover, then tragically relapsed and died because not enough penicillin was

*Top: Third and fourth generations of Lilly, Eli Lilly and Josiah K Lilly, Jr. **Right:** A 1946 view inside one of the the fifteen laboratories used in the control of production.*

available to continue the treatment. The next recipient however was a boy with coxitis who recovered.

Initially the quantities of penicillin being produced were tiny. True industrial production only arrived with American involvement in the second world war. The vast resources of the USA were harnessed to produce penicillin in huge quantities, with Allied casualties in Tunisia and Sicily in 1943 being the first significant groups to benefit from the new antibiotic.

Fleming and Florey were knighted in 1944. In 1945 Fleming, Florey and Chain jointly received the Nobel Prize for Physiology and Medicine.

Meanwhile in 1943 the Ministry of Supply had been looking into the possibility of building a penicillin plant in Britain to match those being built in the USA. The top secret wartime project was known as Job 800.

In 1944, soon after the D-day landings in Europe, a fermentation plant was built at Speke near Liverpool operated by the Distillers Company on behalf of the Ministry of Supply. The new plant was built on a green field site marked only by two enormous bomb craters, reminders of the Luftwaffe's blitz on Liverpool

The plant was an almost exact copy of one in Terre Haute, Indiana in the USA, owned by Commercial Solvents which was also involved in penicillin production.

Speke was ready for operation towards the end of 1945. Batch 0001 was ready for sale by the end of December. Very soon every doctor in the country was able to prescribe penicillin, a previously rare and much sought after medicine, to every patient in need.

The plant was soon being called the biggest penicillin factory in the world. By 1946 the road on which it stood was renamed Fleming Road. Two years later Sir Alexander Fleming himself visited the site and was said to have been moved to tears by what he saw.

The site was selected partly because of its proximity to the railway, though in the end the railway was never used. Additionally however, Merseyside was a plentiful source of labour, whilst Distillers already had three other fermentation plants in the area from where it could draw a skeleton staff of process workers, supervisors and engineers. And there were good supplies of water to hand – critical for use in the fermentation process.

In 1955, the year of Fleming's death, and the tenth anniversary of the first production at Speke, a Fleming memorial was unveiled on the site. In 1979 – the 50th

*Top: The sterile area where girls wearing sterilised clothing and gloves inserted sterilised rubber stoppers in bottle of penicillin, 1946. **Above left:** The Antibiotics Recovery Laboratory in the 1950s.*

anniversary of Fleming's paper on penicillin, Lilly Speke celebrated the connection with a special lunch. The highlight was the starter 'Pate a la Petrie' a brown jelly representing the culture medium, a white surface representing the colony of staphylococci and a green mould for the penicillium - an edible reminder of Fleming's remarkable discovery.

In the early 1950s the Speke plant worked closely with Eli Lilly and Company in Indianapolis, and by the early 1950s started work on one of its new antibiotics - erythromycin. This was another top-secret project. Erythromycin was referred to as Product 322 after the lock number of the building in which it was fermented - the No 3 Fermenter House, still in use today at Speke.

Eli Lilly and Company acquired the Speke plant from Distillers in late 1962 and a new name was introduced on 1st January 1963. For the next three decades the business at Speke would trade under the name of Dista Products rather than under that of Eli Lilly. Lilly had thought of calling the business the Kirby Manufacturing Company after the traditional second name of the Lilly family's sons, though in the end Dista prevailed taking its name from Distaquaine, an important pharmaceutical product.

Now the Speke plant began to concentrate neither on penicillin, nor on any antibiotic for human use but on the fermentation of a new Lilly product 'Tylosin' the world's first antibiotic created exclusively for animal use. The first batch of Tylosin was produced at Speke in August 1963: the next year saw five more Tylosin formulations being fermented at Speke.

The early 1970s saw penicillin production on the Speke site cease entirely. Today, the only antibiotics for human use still being produced at Speke is a drug to treat Multi-Drug Resistant Tuberculosis, capreomycin, distributed at cost price to the World Health Organisation, under the name Capastat.

The biggest boost to Speke in this period however came early in 1964. The Dista marketing division came up with

the name Distalgesic for Dista's new analgesic or painkiller - a name which did more than anything to place the company's own name firmly in the public consciousness.

In 1965 the Lilly concept of 'total quality assurance' was introduced, including the requirement to write all manufacturing instructions into a standard format – or what is called a manufacturing work-ticket. By doing so the company had pre-empted the stringent controls which would be introduced by the Medicines Act of 1968 by three years.

Major upgrades to the plant took place in 1970. Work began on a fourth fermenting house, whilst the old No 1 fermenting house was dismantled. In due course there would only be two large fermenting houses left on site -

Top: An aerial view of the site in the 1950s.
Above: The Fermenter House No 3 computer system pictured in the 1960s.

confusingly to the uninitiated named Nos 3 and 4. Those upgrades were added to in 1980 with an £8.5 million investment in four 30,000 gallon (150,000 litre) fermentation tanks which were viewed by the Duke of Gloucester on a Royal visit to the plant the following year.

Further expansion would involve the production of biosynthetic insulin.

In 1922 in the USA Lilly had become became the first pharmaceutical company in the world to produce insulin on an industrial scale for general use by diabetes sufferers. The insulin was extracted from the pancreatic glands of animals. In 1980, for the first time in history, a diabetic was injected with insulin which had been produced synthetically - using DNA technology or 'genetic engineering' to produce a product, which unlike animal-sourced insulin, was identical in chemical structure to that found in the human body. Dista Products took a key role in fermenting material used for development, clinical work and sales of human insulin, and Dista's lead in biotechnology was announced on 5th April 1982 when the £5 million biosynthetic human insulin plant was officially opened by then Secretary of State for the Environment, the Rt. Hon Michael Heseltine.

Today Lilly's continuing mission is to provide customers with 'Answers that Matter' through innovative medicines, information, and exceptional customer service that enables people to live longer, healthier and more active lives. The company continues to invest tens of millions of pounds in the Speke site, maintaining its high quality and production standards as well as capacity. The products have changed down the years: Lilly Speke Operations now manufactures the entire worldwide supply for the Lilly market of a biosynthetic human growth hormone manufactured using

recombinant DNA technology – a real area of expertise for the site. Today, Lilly Speke are the largest bulk biotechnology manufacturing company in the UK – a position consolidated by the construction of a £50 million state of the art manufacturing facility to make human growth hormone. Additionally, something which the site had manufactured for several decades in small quantities – an antibiotic used to treat Multi-Drug Resistant Tuberculosis - has once again come to the fore as a vital medicine. Multi-Drug Resistant TB is increasing and in 2003, Eli Lilly and Company globally embarked on a public-private partnership to increase the number of trained personnel, the quantity of drugs available and also transfer of technological know-how to countries where the disease is more prevalent. Lilly Speke have doubled their plant capacity with a £5 million investment to stem the tide until the benefits of the Lilly MDR-TB partnership allows China and Russia to locally manufacture this life-saving medicine for themselves.

The company's high reputation does not rest solely on its production strengths: it also aims to be a caring and responsible employer, and one which is part of the local community from which many of its employees come. The company not only hosts an annual event for the local community but also, alongside its staff, actively contributes to many local charities.

Eli Lilly and Company's heritage is one that not only Eli Lilly himself would have been thrilled with, but also one which every person on the Liverpool site who has been involved with the Company through the decades can take equal pride and pleasure.

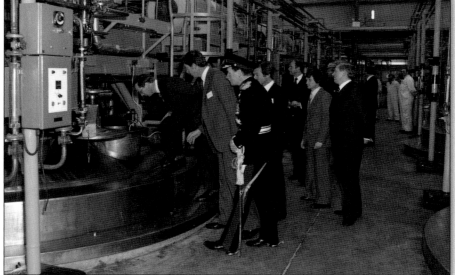

Left: The company's first Royal visit, February 1981. HRH the Duke of Gloucester, cousin to the Queen, spent three hours touring the site.
Above: Operator at work in the newly extended capreomycin facility.

SHOPPING SPREE

Below: We might have been struggling to find tempting goods in the shops in the summer of 1947 as rationing was still a major factor in our lives, but you would not think so from this view along Lord Street, from the corner with Whitechapel. The pavements were thronged with shoppers. Perhaps many of them were just gazing into the windows of shops such as British Home Stores (BHS), Times Furnishing, Wallis's and Hope Brothers as they idly imagined what they could get if only they had enough coupons. Considering that this was 17th July and at the height of a glorious summer, some of the clothing seems incongruous when looking at the state of the weather. People's attire was much more formal back then. When you went out and about in the city it was the done thing for men to wear a jacket and tie and even pop a flat cap on your head if you were one of the older generation. Women usually put on their best coats and not many would think of going out bareheaded. The modern scene would have us in T-shirts, shorts and crop tops with inches of midriff on display. The shop fronts today are more garish and, to the right, include examples of today's lifestyle with Thomson's Holidays, Burger King and Gap occupying the sites, some in new premises. The BHS store has moved to a new block next door and been replaced by Warren James, Swarovski and the Gold Centre.

This junction of Ranelagh Street to the right, with Church Street to the left and Bold Street behind the camera has several points of interest for those who love period pieces. In June 1947, the milk bar was a forerunner of the coffee bars that proliferated in the 1950s and were loved by young adults who enjoyed frothy coffee or Coca-Cola. Today, we have theme bars and wine bars as alcohol has become a must. The Bertram Hayes Seafaring Boys' Club was one of many organisations aimed at the youth of the day, dedicated to uplifting their souls by providing opportunities for healthy exercise. Lager louts need not apply. W Alex Kerr offered ladies' hairdressing. That simplistic term soon became transformed into

'stylist' and the shop became a salon. The Cadbury's van is a reminder of the type of vehicle we collected as Dinky models. If only we had not played with them and kept them in a pristine condition in their original boxes then our pensions would be secure. Models in their original state command large prices at fairs and auctions. The tram was a feature on the city streets for the best part of a century and, just after the war, their disappearance 10 years hence seemed unthinkable. Finally, take note of the Belisha beacons. There are no road markings in the zebra pattern we now know. They were not introduced until the early 1950s. The Disney store, Thomson's, fashion shops and Conlan's opticians have replaced the businesses we used to see here.

EVENTS OF THE 1940s

WHAT'S ON?

In wartime Britain few families were without a wireless set. It was the most popular form of entertainment, and programmes such as ITMA, Music While You Work and Workers' Playtime provided the people with an escape from the harsh realities of bombing raids and ration books. In 1946 the BBC introduced the Light Programme, the Home Service and the Third Programme, which gave audiences a wider choice of listening.

GETTING AROUND

October 1948 saw the production of Britain's first new car designs since before the war. The Morris Minor was destined for fame as one of the most popular family cars, while the four-wheel-drive Land Rover answered the need for a British-made off-road vehicle.

The country was deeply in the red, however, because of overseas debts incurred during the war. The post-war export drive that followed meant that British drivers had a long wait for their own new car.

SPORTING CHANCE

American World Heavyweight Boxing Champion Joe Louis, who first took the title back in 1937, ruled the world of boxing during the 1930s and 40s, making a name for himself as unbeatable. Time after time he successfully defended his title against all comers, finally retiring in 1948 after fighting an amazing 25 title bouts throughout his boxing career. Louis died in 1981 at the age of 67.

The frontage has been remodelled and the name of Boodle and Dunthorne reduced to just Boodles nowadays, but the premises are still intact on the corner of North John Street with Lord Street. The clock continues to tick away and young couples still enter the shop nervously looking for that special token of love that will adorn the third finger, left hand, for the rest of their lives. Pictured in 1948, any lovers choosing wedding rings will soon be coming up to the time when they can celebrate their golden anniversary. How many youngsters in the 21st century can look forward to such an event? Previous generations went through set phases in their relationships. It was boy meets girl, they fall in love, get married, live together and have children. Somewhere along the line our society seems to have reversed part of the order and even left out some of it. The Boodle and Dunthorne shop came to Liverpool in 1798. It was subject to major internal refurbishment earlier this century, under the leadership of designer Eva Jiricna. The £1,000,000 revamp includes a £100,000 'floating' glass staircase and a cocktail lounge where potential buyers can try out diamond rings and necklaces before they buy. The shop has a large window featuring a monthly display about a Liverpool cultural or sporting event, together with educational displays on diamond making

Above: Most of the shops in this part of Queen Square have gone, swept away as this part of the city was redeveloped and the bus station, multi storey car park and St John's Shopping Centre dominated this corner. The Royal Court theatre was thankfully spared and is often in use today for various concerts. In 1962, the music was created outside here by the noise of lorries revving up as they dropped off their loads of fresh produce for the host of greengrocers who earned a living in the vicinity. Before long, of course, these retailers would start to feel the pinch of the supermarket threat. Shopping at individual outlets for our meat, greens, fruit, bread, fish etc was commonplace in the 1960s, but things were to change. There were self service shops in the 1950s, but it was only with the building of the large stores that the squeeze was put on the small, family businesses. The new giants could build large premises that held everything under one roof and was priced at a level that the small shopkeeper found impossible to match. Gradually, more and more of the specialist shops disappeared and the pile 'em high, sell' em cheap brigade swallowed up their clients. Housewives who moaned about the loss of the personal touch they got from their own butcher had only themselves to blame.

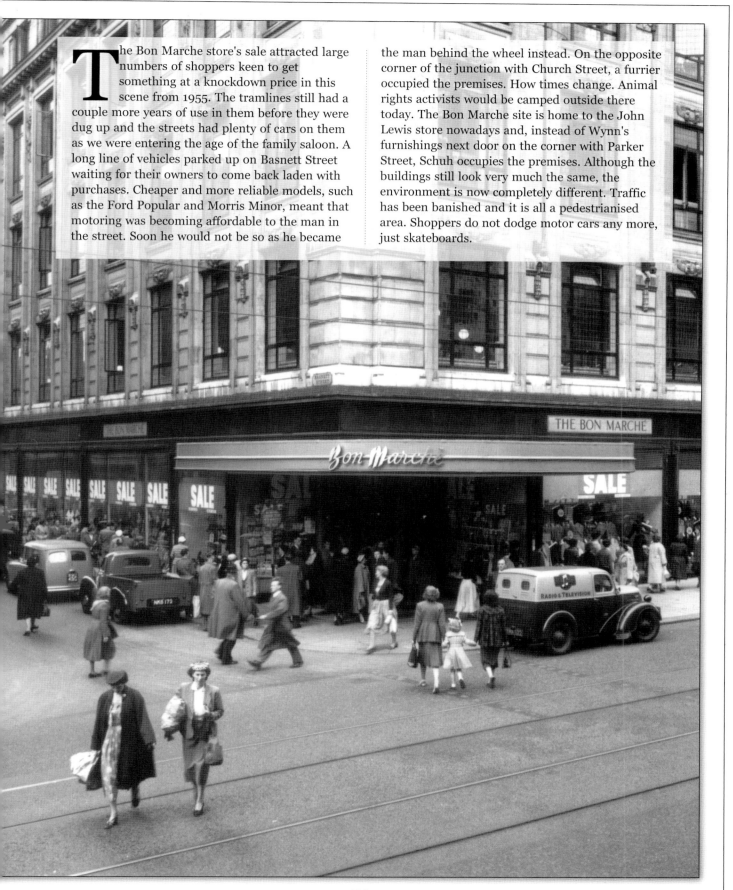

The Bon Marche store's sale attracted large numbers of shoppers keen to get something at a knockdown price in this scene from 1955. The tramlines still had a couple more years of use in them before they were dug up and the streets had plenty of cars on them as we were entering the age of the family saloon. A long line of vehicles parked up on Basnett Street waiting for their owners to come back laden with purchases. Cheaper and more reliable models, such as the Ford Popular and Morris Minor, meant that motoring was becoming affordable to the man in the street. Soon he would not be so as he became the man behind the wheel instead. On the opposite corner of the junction with Church Street, a furrier occupied the premises. How times change. Animal rights activists would be camped outside there today. The Bon Marche site is home to the John Lewis store nowadays and, instead of Wynn's furnishings next door on the corner with Parker Street, Schuh occupies the premises. Although the buildings still look very much the same, the environment is now completely different. Traffic has been banished and it is all a pedestrianised area. Shoppers do not dodge motor cars any more, just skateboards.

Church Street is one of the city's main shopping areas and little has changed in that respect. The stores and retail outlets still do good business, though some of the names on the frontages may have changed. The Barker and Dobson sweetshop on the left now belongs to H Samuel, the jeweller, and the Saxone shoe emporium is a Jane Norman enterprise. The major alteration that strikes anyone visiting this part of the city today is the absence of traffic. Shoppers no longer have to contend with the exhaust fumes that must have caused havoc in the poor bobby's lungs as he spent several hours at a time on point duty. Ensconced in his little box, he held immense power in his arms. With just one imperious gesture he could bring dozens of cars to a halt and, with a simple movement of the wrist, send them on their way again. Not for him the whistles and toots of the American cop or the theatrical antics of a Gallic gendarme; what else did he need other than movements of majesty and clarity? Notice the hemlines in 1955. How they bounce up and down as ladies' whims and fancies change. Just over half a century ago skirt lengths were almost the same as those favoured in Edwardian times.

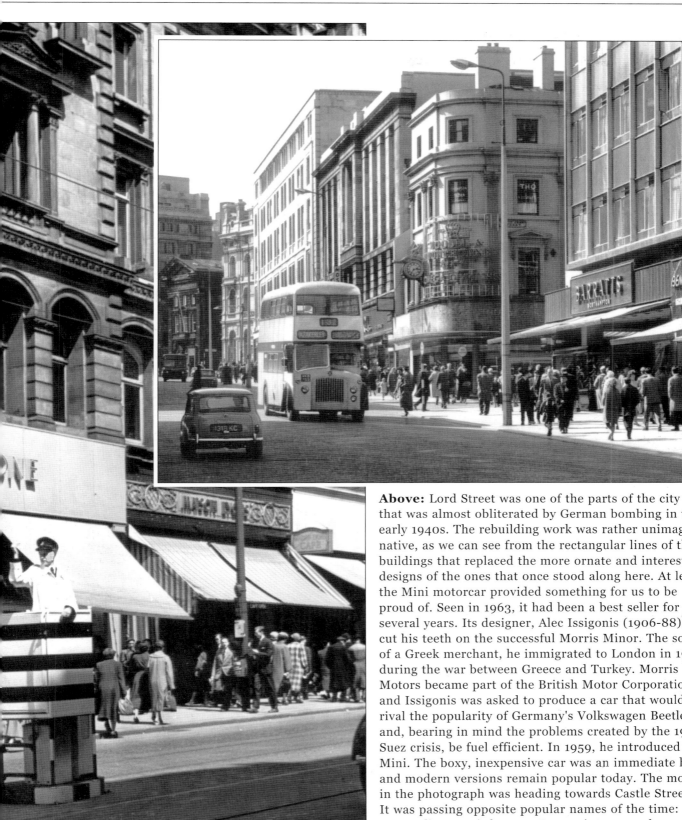

Above: Lord Street was one of the parts of the city that was almost obliterated by German bombing in the early 1940s. The rebuilding work was rather unimaginative, as we can see from the rectangular lines of the buildings that replaced the more ornate and interesting designs of the ones that once stood along here. At least the Mini motorcar provided something for us to be proud of. Seen in 1963, it had been a best seller for several years. Its designer, Alec Issigonis (1906-88), cut his teeth on the successful Morris Minor. The son of a Greek merchant, he immigrated to London in 1922 during the war between Greece and Turkey. Morris Motors became part of the British Motor Corporation and Issigonis was asked to produce a car that would rival the popularity of Germany's Volkswagen Beetle and, bearing in mind the problems created by the 1956 Suez crisis, be fuel efficient. In 1959, he introduced the Mini. The boxy, inexpensive car was an immediate hit and modern versions remain popular today. The model in the photograph was heading towards Castle Street. It was passing opposite popular names of the time: Lennard's, Dunn's hatters, Bennett's camera shop and Barratt's. The bus is level with the corner of North John Street where the Boodle and Dunthorne clock is still a landmark.

Above: The distinctive Bunney's store on Church Street, Whitechapel, attracted hordes of bargain hunters in 1956. According to the large advertising signs, everything had to go and stocks must be cleared in the great reorganisation sale. Queues formed right round the block as a largely female clientele made sure of getting something at a knockdown price. Half a century ago, there were special times when shops had sales. They occurred seasonally and provided traders with an opportunity to offload goods that had stuck on the shelves or needed to be cleared to make way for new or more fashionable lines. In more recent times we have become used to the almost perennial sale status of some stores, especially those selling furniture at the lower end of the market. Those businesses always state that the offers must end on Sunday, but never seem to determine which one they are talking about. Bargain hunters in the middle of the 20th century knew that their opportunities only lasted for a few days and they were happy to wait outside the store for long hours until the doors opened and they could rush in and bag something that they had their eyes on for weeks. Church Street is now pedestrianised, so the sight of cars in this part of the city makes the photograph a true period piece.

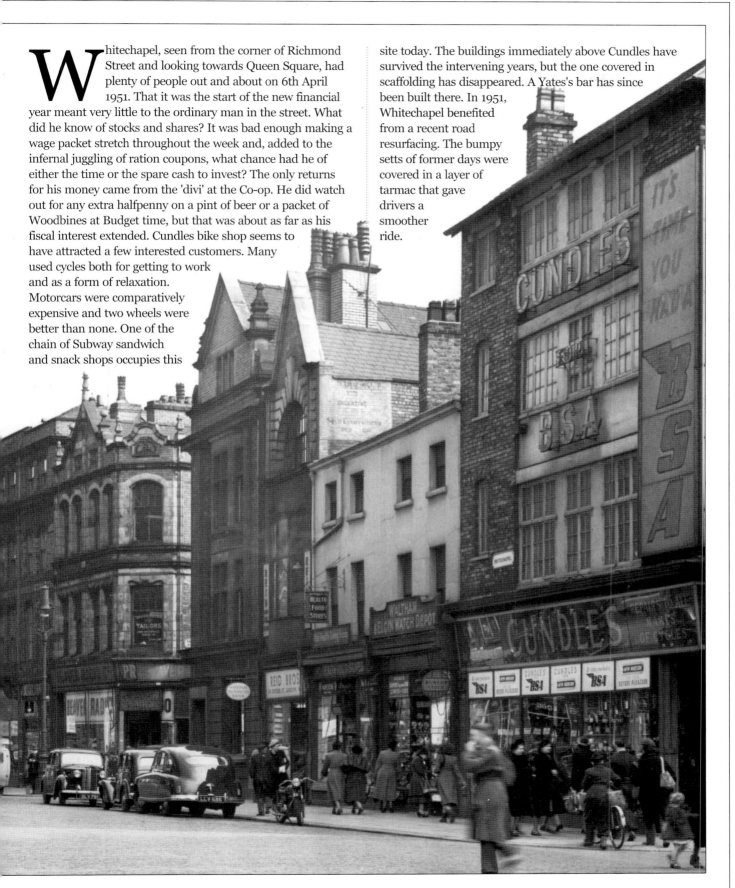

Whitechapel, seen from the corner of Richmond Street and looking towards Queen Square, had plenty of people out and about on 6th April 1951. That it was the start of the new financial year meant very little to the ordinary man in the street. What did he know of stocks and shares? It was bad enough making a wage packet stretch throughout the week and, added to the infernal juggling of ration coupons, what chance had he of either the time or the spare cash to invest? The only returns for his money came from the 'divi' at the Co-op. He did watch out for any extra halfpenny on a pint of beer or a packet of Woodbines at Budget time, but that was about as far as his fiscal interest extended. Cundles bike shop seems to have attracted a few interested customers. Many used cycles both for getting to work and as a form of relaxation. Motorcars were comparatively expensive and two wheels were better than none. One of the chain of Subway sandwich and snack shops occupies this site today. The buildings immediately above Cundles have survived the intervening years, but the one covered in scaffolding has disappeared. A Yates's bar has since been built there. In 1951, Whitechapel benefited from a recent road resurfacing. The bumpy setts of former days were covered in a layer of tarmac that gave drivers a smoother ride.

Left: Standing at the junction of Lord Street with Whitechapel and Paradise Street, the 6A tram had come to a halt outside Hope Brothers' outfitters. This form of transport served the city for nearly 100 years. The first ones were, of course, horse drawn and began operating in November 1869 following an Act of Parliament that granted the Liverpool Tramways Company permission to found this service. Ours was the first city in Europe to run such a system and the initial fleet numbered 16 double decker cars, each seating 46 passengers. This form of transport was immensely popular with the general public, but was wound down after the second world war. Liverpool decided to follow a fashion already set by many other British cities and abandon the trams in favour of buses, despite having an extensive system in place with much of the track running in the central reservations of main roads connecting the city and its suburbs. You can still see and even ride in one of Liverpool's streamliner trams, also known as 'Green Goddesses', at Britain's National Tramway Museum at Crich, in Derbyshire. The last official tram to run on our streets was car 293, which was painted in a special light cream livery for that final journey on 14 September 1957. This tram was sold to the Seashore Trolley Museum in Kennebunkport, Maine in the USA.

Above: The pace of life around Lime Street and Elliot Street was very different in 1963. Today, a simple stroll across the road is impossible with the volume of traffic that now exists. This part of the city has changed almost beyond recognition. Hellewell's, Platt's and the Griddle Hamburger Bar no longer dominate this corner. Instead, that honour now belongs to a Holiday Inn. When this photograph was taken, things were happening on the music scene in the city. Elvis Presley, with only Cliff Richard giving him a run for his money, dominated the pop music charts in the early 60s. But, there were groups of youngsters getting together in smoke-filled clubs in Liverpool who provided a raw, but different, sound from the rockabilly style that Elvis had graduated to and the lightweight stuff Cliff was churning out. At the end of 1962, four mop headed lads had a small hit with 'Love me do'. A year later, Beatlemania was rocking the country and even taking America by storm. Though they were not the first Liverpool group to top the charts, that honour belonging to Gerry and the Pacemakers, John, Paul, George and Ringo were to become synonymous with the term 'Mersey beat' and become the stuff of legends.

STREET SCENES

Looking from the corner at Bold Street, the Adelphi Hotel and Lewis's feature prominently. On the right, modern shops now front the old Central Station on Ranelagh Street, but in this picture we can see its entrance area in all its former glory. Liverpool has its place in railway history firmly established by the trials that took place at Rainhill in 1829, ensuring that George Stephenson's 'Rocket' won the day and the first passenger rail line connecting Liverpool and Manchester could open the following year. Central Station opened as part of the Cheshire Lines Railway's extension of their line into Liverpool's city centre. It had previously terminated at the inconveniently located Brunswick station. This imposing station had a grand three storey façade, behind which was a single arched train shed that reached a height of 65 feet. There were three island platforms giving six platform faces. Within a few years of its opening, Central Station offered services to Manchester, Stockport and Southport. By 1883, the journey time to Manchester was an impressive 40 minutes. The low level platforms that catered for services running deep beneath the River Mersey to Rock Ferry and Birkenhead were opened in 1892. Despite a high volume of traffic, the station was downsized in 1966 under the Beeching reorganisation plans. The high level platforms closed in 1975 and the low levels later became part of the Merseyrail link.

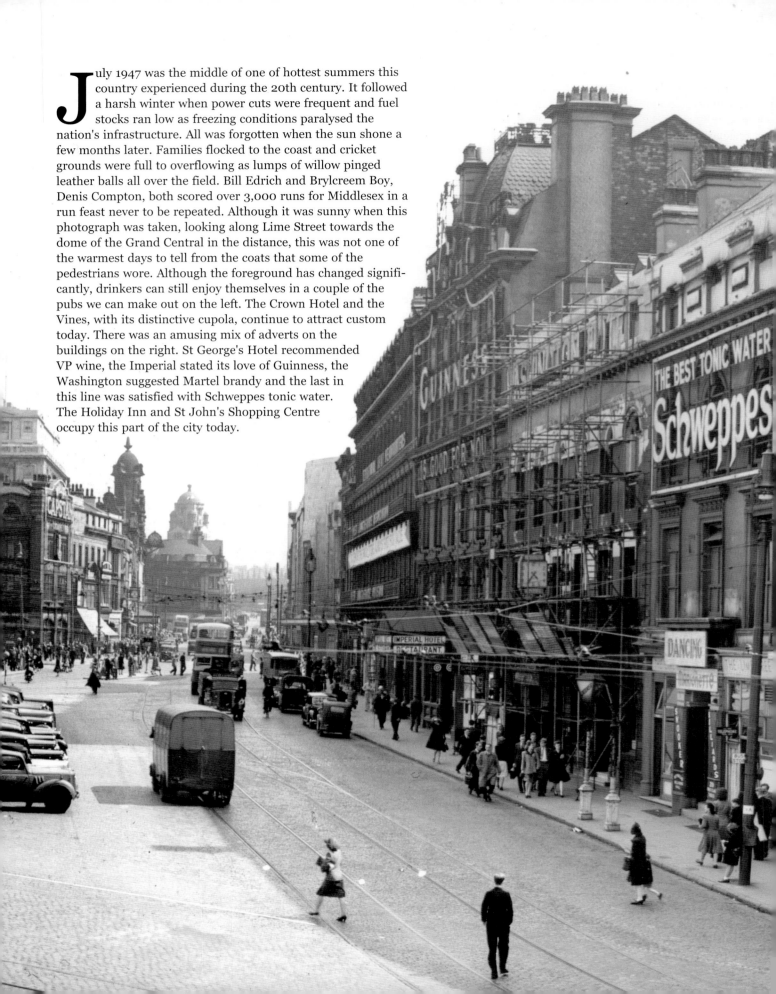

July 1947 was the middle of one of hottest summers this country experienced during the 20th century. It followed a harsh winter when power cuts were frequent and fuel stocks ran low as freezing conditions paralysed the nation's infrastructure. All was forgotten when the sun shone a few months later. Families flocked to the coast and cricket grounds were full to overflowing as lumps of willow pinged leather balls all over the field. Bill Edrich and Brylcreem Boy, Denis Compton, both scored over 3,000 runs for Middlesex in a run feast never to be repeated. Although it was sunny when this photograph was taken, looking along Lime Street towards the dome of the Grand Central in the distance, this was not one of the warmest days to tell from the coats that some of the pedestrians wore. Although the foreground has changed significantly, drinkers can still enjoy themselves in a couple of the pubs we can make out on the left. The Crown Hotel and the Vines, with its distinctive cupola, continue to attract custom today. There was an amusing mix of adverts on the buildings on the right. St George's Hotel recommended VP wine, the Imperial stated its love of Guinness, the Washington suggested Martel brandy and the last in this line was satisfied with Schweppes tonic water. The Holiday Inn and St John's Shopping Centre occupy this part of the city today.

Below: Henry Ford once said that people could have any colour of car that they wanted, as long as it was black. On Castle Street in 1946, the cars on view largely bear out his statement. Of late, silver has been the most popular choice of colour for a new car, but 60 years ago it was a different matter. Cars were meant to be functional, not fashionable. Castle Street is now part of the one way system introduced in the 1960s and the sight of traffic moving freely in both directions, allied with the view of the old tramlines, certainly dates this photograph. Some things remain, thankfully. Despite the best attempts of the German Luftwaffe during the last war, the Town Hall still dominates the Water Street end of this road, though it required considerable repairs after a raid in 1941. The present building is the third to have been built on or near the site. The first made its entrance in 1515 with the second being erected in 1673. The Town Hall as we know it today was built in 1754, based on a design by John Wood of Bath. It was gutted by fire in 1794, but was rebuilt and restored over the following years. The building features a 10 feet high, gold leaf covered statue of Minerva, the goddess of wisdom, among other things, mounted on the dome on the roof. It was designed by Felix Rossi, who was sculptor to George IV.

The plateau in front of St George's Hall on 2nd July 1947 is basically the same as it ever was. The war memorial tomb, Queen Victoria on horseback and the imposing column on which Arthur Wesley (later Wellesley), Duke of Wellington (1769-1852) stands are all still in their rightful places. Similarly, the statue of the Earl of Beaconsfield (1804-81) has remained unmoved by the changes he has seen unfold in front of him. The distinctive Burton's store, typical of the design favoured by this 'tailor of taste', has gone, though the Empire Theatre remains. This building is on the site where the New Prince of Wales Theatre and Opera House was opened on 15th October 1866. It was renamed the Royal Alexandra Theatre and Opera House, in honour of the Princess of Wales, the following year. Under new ownership, it became the Empire Theatre in 1896. It was rebuilt and extended in 1925 and claimed to have the largest stage in Britain, measuring 160 x 40 feet. Many famous names have appeared here, including Bing Crosby and Frank Sinatra. The Beatles' last concert in Liverpool was held here in 1965 before they took a 'Ticket to ride' to bigger auditoriums. The fountain, glimpsed above the Earl's head, was sculpted by Paul Lienard and presented to the city by the former mayor, Lieutenant-Colonel RF Steble, in 1877.

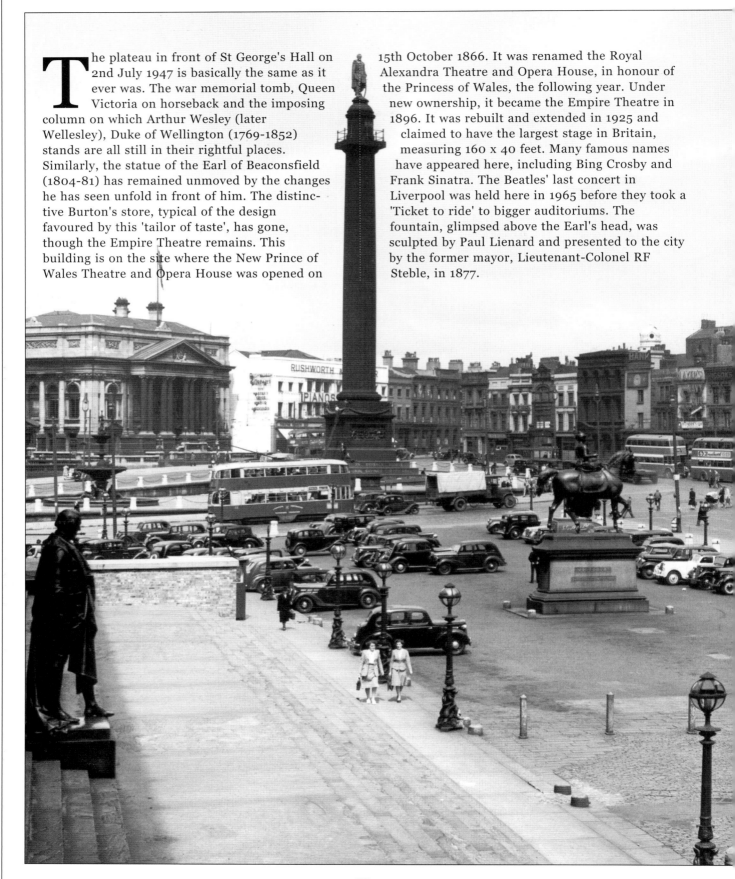

Above: The No Entry sign on Ranelagh Street meant little to the German bombers that flew in during May 1941. They dropped their hail of fire on the city below during that most traumatic of months when Britain's heartlands were battered night after night at the height of the blitz. Liverpool, London, Belfast, Glasgow, Southampton and Hull were among the worst hit, but no site of industry or major centre of population was immune. When the dust finally settled, the nation counted the cost, but rebuilding could not take place on a large scale until after the war. The process of regeneration was to be a long and drawn out affair. Those growing up in the baby boomer years of the late 1940s were well accustomed to seeing huge tracts of wasteland that remained as empty bombsites for years to come. The 1908 Blackler's department store, centre, one of Liverpool's most popular shops, was less fortunate than some of its neighbour. The building was completely destroyed by fire in the air raid and, although rebuilding work began in 1950, it was not until 1955 that the work was fully completed.

Below: The light coloured building that dominates the centre right of this November 1947 photograph is now 151 Dale Street and is named Stanley House. Many locals still refer to it as Blackburn House as it is the former home of the Blackburn Assurance Company. It was established primarily to deal with events that were certain or assured to happen and, therefore, concentrated on life policies. It might have had to pay out to the occupants of the cortege making its way out of the entrance to the tunnel. A hearse and several mourners' cars were making their way towards the city centre. Liverpool had seen more than its fair share of grief in the immediately preceding years. Funeral processions became sadly commonplace after an air raid. Death in peacetime seemed that bit sadder as the poor soul who had just passed away had escaped all that Hitler's mob had hurled his way, but had hardly survived long enough to enjoy the freedom that victory brought. Even if he had done, the hearse would have been one of the few means of transport open to him. Petrol was heavily rationed and private motorists struggled to stay on the road for more than a few miles at a time.

Above: This from was taken from Martin's Bank in June 1947. Along the right hand side of the roadway are some of the many fine, distinctive buildings that distinguish our city. The statue of Minerva is functional as well as decorative. She acts as a lightning conductor in addition to her roles as the Roman goddess of knowledge, the arts, wisdom and war. She was obviously a many faceted lady, but we all know that women are wonderfully adept at multi tasking. Minerva sits atop the Town Hall that was completed in 1811, just one of several that has served the city over time. The Town Hall was the centre of civic and mercantile activity at that time. The less than savoury slave trade provided a considerable portion of the city's wealth. By 1795 Liverpool controlled over 80 per cent of the British and over 40 per cent of the entire European slave trade. The majority of the mayors who strode the Town Hall floor over the years that slavery was legal had major connections with this lucrative trade. Narrow lanes run off Dale Street from either side, giving some sense of how it would have looked at the height of this shameful business, though this street layout is much older, in parts dating from the medieval period.

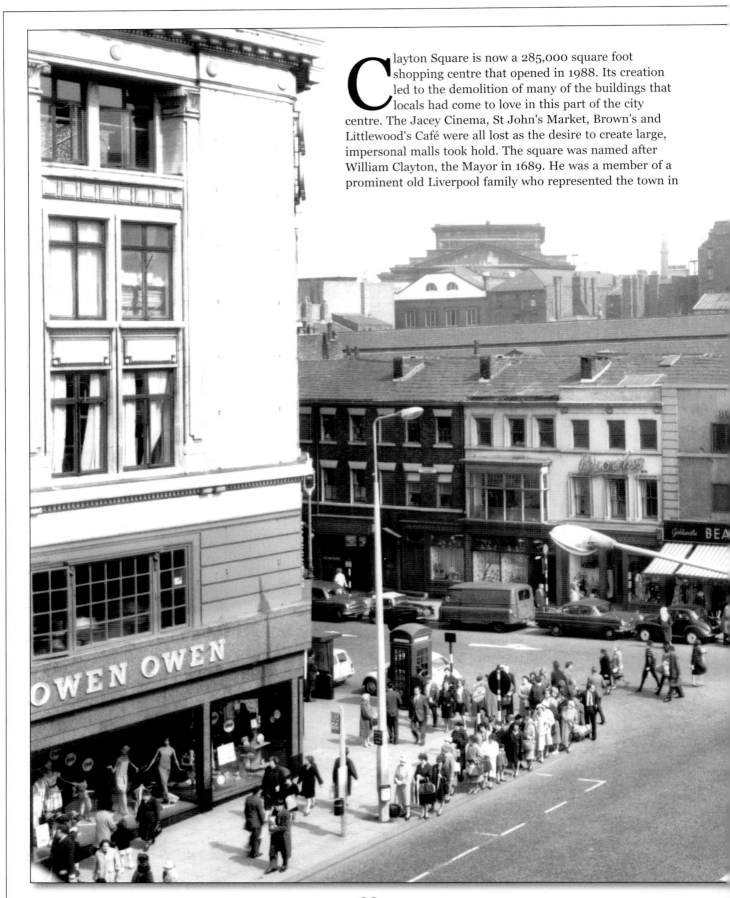

Clayton Square is now a 285,000 square foot shopping centre that opened in 1988. Its creation led to the demolition of many of the buildings that locals had come to love in this part of the city centre. The Jacey Cinema, St John's Market, Brown's and Littlewood's Café were all lost as the desire to create large, impersonal malls took hold. The square was named after William Clayton, the Mayor in 1689. He was a member of a prominent old Liverpool family who represented the town in eight parliaments between the years 1698 and 1714. The square was laid out between 1745 and 1750 and named in his honour. In 1769 only four houses are recorded as existing here and one of these was converted into the Prince of Wales Theatre that was demolished in 1912. In keeping with the new craze for cinema, the Liverpool Picture House was built adjacent to the site. It changed its name on numerous occasions over the years to include the Prince of Wales News and

Feature Theatre, the Liverpool News Theatre and Gala Theatre among its metamorphoses. Its final reincarnation found it screening 'adult' films as the Jacey Film Theatre before closing in 1972. The building then underwent a radical transformation into a church, known as the Shrine of the Blessed Sacrament. Many of the surrounding properties, once upon a time grand houses and then prestigious shops, became occupied by budget retail outlets.

Below: The face of Central Station is now greatly changed as shops now front the former imposing entrance. The rail link with Manchester is now accessed via escalators that take passengers deep underground to where there is also a connection with Birkenhead through the Mersey Tunnel. The advert for Mothers Pride, bread 'like mother used to bake', reminds us of the time when mums really did roll up their sleeves and end up with flour up to their armpits as they kneaded, shaped and proofed the mix that turned into delicious cobs, cottage loaves and soda bread. Mothers Pride is still the number one standard bread brand for British Bakeries, part of the Rank Hovis McDougall empire. It made its first appearance in the north in 1936 and became a national brand in 1956. In the late 1970s and 1980s, Mothers Pride was the number one white bread brand and, although recent years have seen the rise in popularity of premium breads, today it is the fourth largest in the UK. Originally it was sold wrapped in wax paper but, as packaging technology progressed, it was packed in bags. Nostalgia buffs will also enjoy the sign promoting Waring and Gillow, the top notch furniture maker. Robert Gillow (1704-72), the company's founding father, used his apprenticeship as a ship's carpenter when he set up business in Lancaster. The company merged with SJ Waring in 1903, but itself was the subject of a takeover in 1961.

Queen Victoria somehow escaped the bombs that fell in May 1941. Quite how her statue remained standing is a mystery, but perhaps the Luftwaffe pilots had some sort of respect for the statue of the woman who was a member of the House of Hanover. Since that is too fanciful, let us just put it down to 'how dare they bomb the grand old queen?' Not much else in the vicinity of Derby Square was left unscathed and here we are looking into what remained of South Castle Street. Air raids were a constant fear in the early 1940s. The country knew what to expect from newsreel footage of the Spanish Civil War when villages and towns were hammered with the help of the Condor Division of the German Air Force sent to help General Franco's power grab. Even so, nothing could truly prepare us for the sheer horror of what was to be unleashed upon our cities as wave after wave of Junkers and Heinkels darkened the skies. Sirens wailed and the population rushed off into Anderson shelters, cellars and even the open countryside. Many were caught unawares by the speed and ferocity of the aerial assaults and perished in their homes and workplaces. Those who were safe often returned to houses that were just burning shells, not homes that they shared with their families. Liverpool was one of Germany's major targets. With its docks and heavy industry vital to the war effort, the Nazis targeted it in earnest. They smashed our city, but did not break our spirit.

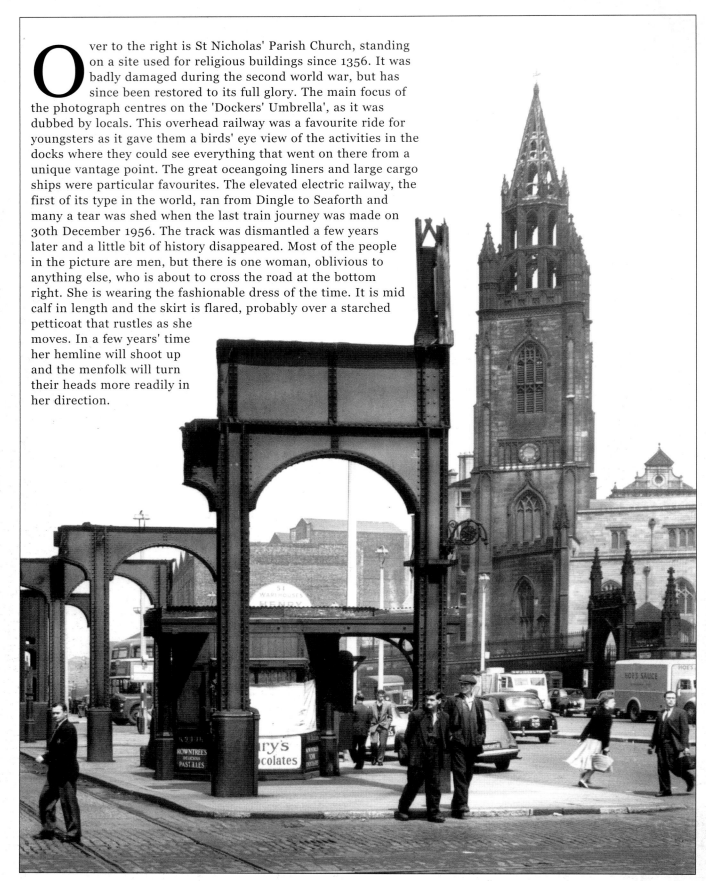

Over to the right is St Nicholas' Parish Church, standing on a site used for religious buildings since 1356. It was badly damaged during the second world war, but has since been restored to its full glory. The main focus of the photograph centres on the 'Dockers' Umbrella', as it was dubbed by locals. This overhead railway was a favourite ride for youngsters as it gave them a birds' eye view of the activities in the docks where they could see everything that went on there from a unique vantage point. The great oceangoing liners and large cargo ships were particular favourites. The elevated electric railway, the first of its type in the world, ran from Dingle to Seaforth and many a tear was shed when the last train journey was made on 30th December 1956. The track was dismantled a few years later and a little bit of history disappeared. Most of the people in the picture are men, but there is one woman, oblivious to anything else, who is about to cross the road at the bottom right. She is wearing the fashionable dress of the time. It is mid calf in length and the skirt is flared, probably over a starched petticoat that rustles as she moves. In a few years' time her hemline will shoot up and the menfolk will turn their heads more readily in her direction.

Even in November 1950 Dale Street was a very busy part of the city. Traffic congestion is not something that is restricted to the modern era, though in the middle of the last century quite a fair proportion of it could be attributed to public transport. Both buses and trams vied for their own particular portion of the carriageway. It is ironic to think that 50 years after the latter were phased out, they may soon be returning to Liverpool. Merseytravel eventually hopes to construct a three line system in the city to service the main corridors into the centre, as well as large residential areas. All three lines will share a loop line around the city centre from Kings Dock through the Albert Dock and then onto Wapping where it will separate. One section will connect Paradise Street to Lime Street, the other Water Street to William Brown Street. Both lines then meet at London Road and at the entrance to the Birkenhead tunnel. This photograph was taken looking across Manchester Street from the direction of the access to the Queensway tunnel and towards Minton's paints shop and the Sterling Boot Company. At this point in time we were halfway through the century that had brought us a mixture of good and evil. We had the benefits of penicillin and other medical advances, but had also experienced the carnage of two world wars

A policeman in a white coat controlled the traffic movement on Dale Street in September 1952 at a time when public transport was still the main way in which Liverpudlians got into and out of the city, whether to work or to shop. It was also a time when hints of the future could be discovered by looking carefully at some current events. In America, both candidates for the presidency, Eisenhower and Stevenson, spoke about equal rights for citizens, irrespective of the colour of their skin. Fine words, but it took another decade before a president would meet the issue head on and he only lasted three years before being assassinated. Double standards, it seemed, were being preached across the pond. Civil rights did not extend to those who rocked the conservatism of America. Senator McCarthy still led the witchhunt for those who practised 'un-American activities' as he railed against 'pinkos' and looked for reds under every bed. Even Charlie Chaplin was under threat. Here, on Dale street, there was no sign of a cold war or race riots. Not that anyone would dare as, just opposite the 1886 Prudential building, the Magistrates' Court can be found on the right!

PRESTON STREET

CHEMIST

Above: In 1953, Britain celebrated the early days of a new Elizabethan era, or so it hoped. We needed something to brighten the grey days of postwar austerity and a new monarch on the throne, following her father's death in 1952, meant that the nation could give itself an excuse to party. Elizabeth II was crowned at Westminster Abbey on 2nd June 1953. It was a wonderful early summer for the British. Everyone outside Bolton had earlier rejoiced that Stan Matthews had, at long last, gained his FA Cup medal in a memorable display for Blackpool. Edmund Hillary stood on top of Everest and we could be proud to wave the flag. The crowds out in Liverpool on this bright day were not celebrating anything special, however. They were just enjoying the panorama, looking across the docks and out to sea. Below them was a testament to the genius of British engineering. Looking like some form of elongated gangplank, this was the old Floating Road. Goods vehicles and cars accessing the ferries were able to use it to get from George's Dock gates down to the landing stage. At ebb tide, the road climbed steeply into the city, but traffic could use it in safety as it floated securely on the river, whatever the state of the tide.

Traces of the tram system could still be seen on Lime Street in November 1959, but it was more than two years earlier that they had last been pressed into use. The familiar sight of the bobby on point duty would disappear as traffic lights were introduced and he remains in our memories as a particular icon of life on city streets nearly 50 years ago. Looking along the road from the Grove Hotel towards Renshaw Street, our eyes and thoughts are immediately occupied by the Forum Cinema. It was part of our formative youth and how sad it is today to see it standing forlorn. It was on the back seats here where we had our first private cuddle and where a bespectacled beau would take off his specs and ask, 'Are we watching the film or what?' Needless to say, he did not get as far as 'what' on a first date. Even then, the eagle-eyed, spoilsports of usherettes shone their torches across the back rows to make sure that there was a distinct lack of hanky and not a chance of panky. The movie on show back then was 'Yesterday's Enemy', a story of suspense set in Burma during the last war. It starred three fine stalwarts of the British film industry in Stanley Baker, Leo McKern and Gordon Jackson.

EVENTS OF THE 1950s

THE WORLD AT LARGE

Plans to develop the economies of member states into one common market came to fruition on 1st January 1958, when the EEC came into operation. The original members were France, Belgium, Luxembourg, The Netherlands, Italy, and West Germany. The Community became highly successful, achieving increased trade and prosperity across Western Europe while at the same time alleviating fear of war which lingered on after the end of World War II. Britain became a member in 1973.

ROYAL WATCH

King George VI's health had been causing problems since 1948, when he developed thrombosis. In 1951 the King - always a heavy smoker - became ill again, and was eventually found to be suffering from lung cancer. His left lung was removed in September of 1951. In January 1952 he waved Princess Elizabeth and Prince Philip off on their tour of Africa; they were never to see him again. The King died on 5th February 1952.

MELODY MAKERS

Few teenage girls could resist the blatant sex-appeal of 'Elvis the Pelvis', though their parents were scandalised at the moody Presley's provocatively gyrating hips. The singer took America and Britain by storm with such hits as 'Jailhouse Rock', 'All Shook Up' and 'Blue Suede Shoes'. The rhythms of Bill Haley and his Comets, Buddy Holly, Chuck Berry, and Roy Orbison (who had a phenomenal three-octave voice) turned the 1950s into the Rock 'n' Roll years.

Below: Someone with a head for heights took this photograph in June 1958. To achieve the camera angle required to produce such an image, he scaled the Wellington Column and aimed his lens along London Road. There we can clearly make out the Odeon Cinema. The film that attracted audiences on this occasion was called 'Gideon's Day'. It was a yarn about an ordinary but frustrating day in the life of a police inspector from Scotland Yard. It is not a movie that immediately brings back any major memories, but most older readers will recall the series of crime books from that era, written by John Creasey as JJ Carric, on which it was based. Gideon of the Yard featured in over 20 novels that were published at the rate of one per year from 1956 onwards. The cast list of 'Gideon's Day' throws up some interesting names. Jack Hawkins, an actor who later lost his voice to cancer, took the star role. Cyril Cusack, one of a dynasty of actors, and a young Andrew Ray took supporting parts. The latter was the son of top comedian Ted Ray who was born in Wigan but raised from an infant in Liverpool. Cinemagoers leaving the Odeon could have nipped into the nearby Legs of Man after the film was over. It was undergoing a facelift at the time and we can see workmen on the roof of the building on the corner with Lime Street.

Above: This elevated view of Dale Street was taken in 1960. A couple of Morris Travellers are making their way along the road. Their owners would not know it, but these examples of British engineering developed a cult ownership. The distinctive wooden trim on the coachwork and the squarish shape to its body, allied to the Morris Minor chassis and engine, marked it out as something special to behold. However, it was not just the look that made these cars popular with owners and, later, collectors. They were reliable and very roadworthy, though this was hardly surprising as the award winning Alec Issigonis designed them. There are a number of distinctive and impressive buildings to be seen on Dale Street. They include the Prudential building, the offices of the Royal Insurance group and the municipal building with its imposing clock tower. To the left, we can make out the entrance to the first Mersey Tunnel. In 1922 a committee, chaired by Sir Archibald Salvidge the main driving force behind the project, was set up to draw up plans for a river crossing. It was probably intended as much for business use as for motorists. The ferries and railway could cope with the passengers, but they could not manage goods traffic efficiently. Work began in 1925, but the tunnel was not officially opened until 1934.

WORKING LIFE

Below: English Electric was one of Merseyside's major employers either side of the last war. It had diverse interests, being involved in the manufacture of large diesel engines, locomotives, aero engines, television parts, radio valves, washing machines and refrigerators. It was taken over by GEC in 1968, something it had done to other, smaller companies in preceding years. During World War II, the country relied heavily on its women to move from stereotyped jobs into those more associated with men. When they went off to join up, the so-called weaker sex took over at heavy engineering plants and worked with large, cumbersome machinery. Elsewhere, they drove buses, repaired roads and got the harvest in. When peace was declared, many refused to give up their jobs. They had become used to getting a regular pay packet and did not want to rely on hubby's generosity with the housekeeping. Perhaps just as important, they had a level of independence and self esteem that had previously been denied to them. These women, pictured in 1948, had no intention of letting go. Some had other reasons to continue working, as they were the sole breadwinners if their loved ones had paid the ultimate price on some foreign field. So, they donned their industrial gloves and put their backs into it and took pride in a job well done.

Row upon row of women sat at the conveyor belts that carried the toys that made every little lad in the land happy. No back bedroom was complete without a collection of Dinky cars. Models of vans, lorries, saloons and the latest Grand Prix racing cars adorned the window sills and lay scattered across the floor. Uttering 'brrm, brrm' as they shoved the Dinkies across the lino, these lads imagined that they were really driving the Pickfords removal van or the delivery wagon that had Lyons Swiss Roll emblazoned on the side. Best of all, though, were the imagined Grand Prix races with model Ferraris, HWMs, Maseratis and Gordinis. Lost in a world of Juan Fangio, Stirling Moss and Mike Hawthorn, children could entertain themselves for hours on end. Just as Hoover became synonymous with the vacuum cleaner, so Dinky became the word for any toy car. The largely female workforce at the Binns Road factory chatted about their Saturday night out as they boxed up the toy cars. Some had already started their preparations for the weekend, keeping their hair curlers covered by headscarves so that their crowning glories would be at their best for an evening at the dance hall. In the background, popular music of the day or the jokes of Charlie Chester could be heard coming over the airwaves as 'Workers' Playtime' was broadcast.

Below: Anyone who has never owned a train set has suffered the greatest child abuse imaginable. Where would we be as youngsters without the opportunity to go 'chuff-chuff' or 'whoo'? Ever since Mr Stephenson set us under way with his 'Rocket' in 1830, the British have had a fascination for railways both large and small. Frank Hornby (1863-1936) is probably the most famous name in toy making. He was brought up a Methodist and met his wife, Clara, when they were members of the Liverpool Philharmonic Society choir. They married in 1887 and had two sons, Roland and Douglas, and a daughter Patricia. To keep his sons happy, Frank made a toy crane out of perforated metal strips held together with nuts and bolts. When the boys asked him to make something else, Hornby undid the pieces and created a different machine from the same bits. He saw a future for this versatile toy and set to work producing it for the mass market. Meccano was born. After the First World War Hornby began making clockwork trains and introduced the first railway engines in 1920 as construction kits. By 1925 all his trains and accessories were sold ready assembled. Here, at Binns Lane in 1950, the women worked with precision tools to turn out the locomotives that have given successive generations endless pleasure. Some of us having never stopped playing with them.

Above: GW Collins was a food packaging company used by many of the leading brands. Here, in 1951, a mainly female workforce packed up such diverse products as Daddie's Sauce and Jacob's Cream Crackers. Some foods were still subject to rationing and the books of coupons would be needed for another three years. This was the price of victory, it seemed, for those who had suffered six years of privation in the war. As they parcelled up the goods these women wondered, now that peacetime had lasted as long as the hostilities, quite why they had to put up with such austere measures. After all, who was it who had actually won the war? Since the country had booted out Churchill in the general election held during the summer of 1945 things seemed to have improved little. The new government introduced the National Health Service and that appeared to be working, but not much else was. In fact, in some quarters, things were getting worse. At the start of the year, Whitehall actually reduced the meat ration to the lowest it had ever been. Since it now stood at just under 1s 6d (7.5p) per person, each individual's allowance would only buy a quarter of a pound of meat per week. By the end of the year, the general public had given up on Labour and brought an ageing Churchill back to power.

Below: The machine operator kept her hair neat and tidy in a turban style headscarf. This could either be to protect her curlers or, simply, to keep out the grease and grime. Her large boots were not intended to be worn in the interests of safety, but simply to keep her tootsies warm on the cold floor. Looking carefully into the box by her feet, we can spot perforated metal strips. Anyone with a passing knowledge of Liverpool's manufacturing history will instantly recognise these as bits of Meccano. They were being turned out at Hornby's Binns Road factory just after the second world war. Hornby began to manufacture his own parts in a small one-room factory at 10-12 Duke Street in the first decade of the last century. He later took premises in Tuebrook but these soon proved to be too small to cope with the demand for his invention. He then bought land in the Old Swan area and opened the Binns Road factory in 1914. This became the company headquarters for more than 60 years. By 1922, Meccano kits of various sizes and costs were available. At its peak, the Meccano system consisted of over 300 pieces and inspired a generation of boys to take up technical careers. During the 1920s and 1930s Meccano Ltd was the biggest toy manufacturer in Britain and in its heyday had factories in Speke and Aintree, as well as manufacturing bases in Argentina, France, Germany, the USA and Spain.

Above: The work was fiddly without being particularly technical. Assembling doorknobs was not exactly rocket science, but it was better than being stuck inside a noisy mill or engineering plant where huge turbines hammered away in a deafening manner all day long. These women on the 1948 production line could while away the hours indulging in light conversation. Most of it centred on the husband and the kids, though the younger ones who were not fettered by such family ties were eager to discuss what they were going to do at the weekend. Friday and Saturday nights were great releases from the day to day toil. A night out at the pictures, perhaps watching 'Brighton Rock' with that nice looking young actor Richard Attenborough in the leading role, would be worth a try. Afterwards, it would be a quick call at the fish and chip shop for a supper wrapped in newspaper and swimming in vinegar. The salt stung on chapped lips, but the food was tasty, nonetheless. Saturday night was for dancing. The Locarno, now the Liverpool Olympia, on West Derby Road was a popular haunt. Just a couple of strides away, lovers of the terpsichorean art (the posh term for dancing used by people who live in Cheshire) could indulge themselves at the Grafton. Top bands such as Joe Loss, Victor Sylvester and even Duke Ellington have played there.

On Saturday night we sit at home watching some brainless television quiz programme where the contestants have been selected on the basis of the more stupid they are then the greater chance they have of being selected to take part. The sole reason for putting ourselves through this is to see if our six numbers have come up on the National Lottery. Of course they never do, so we have to suffer the same performance the following week and put up with 'Casualty' afterwards, just to make it worse. We had the same sort of dreams of getting lucky when we were younger. Then, our hopes centred upon the football pools. Just after five o'clock we tuned into radio's 'Sports' Report', copy coupon in hand, all ready to check if our eight selections would turn out to be drawn games. If so, we could do as Viv Nicholson famously did with her big win in 1961 and 'spend, spend, spend'. Hers was a famous case of rags to riches and back to rags that took her through five husbands, fast cars, bankruptcy and booze. She woke up spent. Seen here in 1948, rows and rows of checkers sat at tables laboriously going through the punters' entry coupons. They were employed by Littlewoods, the top pools' company founded by John Moores.

EVENTS OF THE 1940s

THE WORLD AT LARGE

The desert area of Alamogordo in New Mexico was the scene of the first atomic bomb detonation on July 16th, 1945. With an explosive power equal to more than 15,000 tons of TNT, the flash could be seen 180 miles away.

President Truman judged that the bomb could secure victory over Japan with far less loss of US lives than a conventional invasion, and on 6th August the first of the new weapons was dropped on Hiroshima. Around 80,000 people died.

ROYAL WATCH

By the end of World War II, the 19-year-old Princess Elizabeth and her distant cousin Lieutenant Philip Mountbatten RN were already in love. The King and Queen approved of Elizabeth's choice of husband, though they realised that she was rather young and had not mixed with many other young men. The engagement announcement was postponed until the Princess had spent four months on tour in Africa. The couple's wedding on 20th November 1947 was a glittering occasion - the first royal pageantry since before the war.

MELODY MAKERS

The songs of radio personalities such as Bing Crosby and Vera Lynn were whistled, sung and hummed everywhere during the 1940s. The 'forces' sweetheart' brought hope to war-torn Britain with 'When the Lights go on Again', while the popular crooner's 'White Christmas' is still played around Christmas time even today.

Who can forget songs like 'People Will Say we're in Love', 'Don't Fence Me In', 'Zip-a-dee-doo-dah', and 'Riders in the Sky'?

In Glasgow this would have been called 'the steamie', but it was just the public washhouse to Liverpudlian housewives. These 1952 housewives did not have the advantage of twin tubs and tumble dryers that would become standard equipment in the houses that their children would one day live in. Reddened hands and aching backs characterised the traditional Monday washday. It is easy enough to put a pile of washing into the machine, programme it and leave it while carrying out other jobs, knowing that automation will complete the task without any further help. But these workers knew little of that form of technology, though some wash houses by this time had large tubs, hot dryers, presses and piped hot water. Nor was there any such thing as a créche for their offspring. The baby was put in the pram, brought into the washhouse and left there, at the far end of the building, until the basket was full and it was time to go home and make tea for the men in the house. Liverpool had its first washhouse on Picton Road in 1842 and for some women the weekly visit became a form of social occasion when they could gossip and pass the time of day, while mopping the sweat from their brows.

Below: When you hear about spin these days it usually conjures up a vision of Shane Warne bamboozling any batsman from Mike Gatting onwards. Conversely, the word is often used to refer to the silver tongues of politicians and their aides who attempt to turn a crisis into a victory. But, this pair of shipyard workers knew nothing of the leggies of the Wizard of Oz or the oily words of PR men; they were literally spinning their own yarns. Just as their forebears did on the great sailing ships in the 1800s, they told stories to one another as they worked away, thus giving rise to the phrase that became part of our expressive language. They pooh-poohed the wearing of industrial gloves as their gnarled and calloused hands were tough enough to deal with the thickest of ropes and cables that they used. These were the sorts of men who cut pieces of old twist from a lump of tobacco and shoved them into their pipes to enjoy the satisfying smoke that would make a normal man pale at the thought. They were part of a tough breed, but you had to be to survive long, arduous hours out in all elements. Before nationalisation of the docks, the workers were usually employed on a casual basis that meant reporting for duty in the morning in the hope of being selected.

The Port of Liverpool and
The Mersey Docks & Harbour Company

Liverpool has been a port since the time of King John who chose to use the sheltered creek to embark his troops for Ireland. In 1207 he promised privileges to those who would settle on the Mersey shore where fishermen kept their boats and the occasional vessel arrived from Wales or Ireland to trade in cattle hides, salt and tar.

Today that small creek has disappeared under the city's famous Pier Head. The Port of Liverpool stretches for four miles of docks down river and has another three miles of berths across the Mersey at Birkenhead. Nearly 2,000 acres make up the port and are largely owned by The Mersey Docks and Harbour Company, a comparatively young firm but with a long pedigree and an impressive record of transforming a struggling maritime centre into a thriving shipping and trading community.

Today, the Port of Liverpool handles more cargo than at any time in its history - nearly 34 million tonnes a year. Liverpool is the major UK port for container trade with North America, Britain's major port for imports of grain, for exports of scrap metal, one of Northern Europe's top 10 container ports and the major British port for that trade which first prompted King John's interest, the flow of freight - and people - across the Irish Sea. In a history which has seen peaks and troughs in Liverpool's maritime importance, trade with Ireland has remained a constant feature. During just three months of 1586 sixteen vessels entered the port, all from Irish ports, with linen yarn for the looms of Manchester and hides for tanning in Liverpool. In the same period 17 ships sailed for Ireland carrying varied cargoes - textiles from Manchester, knives and scythes from Sheffield, pewter goods, saddles, soap and 1,400 tennis balls and 14 raquets. The same pattern of

opened to shipping in 1715 after 5 years of work. More docks followed as did the construction of roads and inland waterways. Liverpool prospered from trade with the British West Indies and the American colonies. A late comer to the triangular trade of cheap goods to Africa, slaves to the sugar plantations and sugar, rum and tobacco home to England, Liverpool nevertheless came to dominate the slave trade until its abolition in 1807. The growth of the United States of America provided Liverpool with growing volumes of trade and new docks opened on the Mersey in quick succession - Canning 1828, Clarence 1830, Brunswick 1832, Waterloo 1834, Victoria and Trafalgar 1836, Coberg 1840, Toxteth 1842 and Albert Dock in 1845. The renowned architect and engineer Jesse Hartley was responsible for some of these. On the Cheshire side

imported raw materials and exported manufactured goods is reflected in the Port of Liverpool's global trade of today.

In the early part of the 17th century Liverpool claimed its share of the trade with the newly founded colonies beyond the seas and finally overhauled the competing port of Chester. By the middle of the century Liverpool had become the undoubted northern port for Ireland and by the latter half claimed to be the third port of England, further stimulated by the opening of direct trade with the American colonies and especially the West Indies.

The Plague of London in 1665 followed by the Great Fire the next year combined with the insecurity of southern waters during the Dutch wars to assist Liverpool as London merchants sought a new base for their trade. Preferences for the port increased with the French wars which made it safer to ship goods from America to Liverpool and by land to London rather than run the gauntlet of the French pirates who infested the English Channel. With as many as 60 or 70 ships of 50 to 200 tons in Liverpool at the time of William III, thoughts were given to the construction of the port's first dock to ease the precarious task of loading and discharging cargoes in the strong tides and storms of the river or pool. Built by Thomas Steers, the enclosed dock with its own gates, was

of the river, the first docks were opened in 1847 around a natural inlet known as the Wallasey Pool - the counterpart of the pool of Liverpool, sparking a period of competition between the two banks of the Mersey until in 1855, Liverpool Corporation then purchased the undertakings of the Birkenhead Dock Trustees, bringing the control of docks at both Liverpool and Birkenhead under one authority.

In 1857 on the recommendation of a Royal Commission, the Mersey Docks and Harbour Board consisting of members elected by the dock ratepayers, became the governing body of both property and the power to collect dues, and remained so until 1971 - the year it was succeeded by the Mersey Docks and Harbour Company. Meanwhile, Liverpool's prestige increased and in 1881 the Prince and Princess of Wales sailed in to open the Langton Dock entrance and name the Alexandra Dock. In 1893 the Liverpool Overhead Railway, an electric, elevated passenger transport system which carried dockers, seafarers and sightseers above the teeming and congested traffic of the Dock Road between the city centre and the docks, was officially opened from Herculaneum Dock in the south to Alexandra Dock in the north. A year later it was extended to take in the residential areas of Seaforth and Waterloo in the north and then as far as Dingle in the south. The "Overhead" which ran parallel with the river for over six miles, gave its passengers a bird's eye view of busy dock scenes which in the year 1900 reflected Liverpool's position as one of the country's most important ports. The value of goods passing through was estimated at £207 million and 2,085 vessels with a total tonnage of over 2

Left: Busy scene at Liverpool landing stage.
Above: Cargoes of coal moving by ship, train and horse drawn cart.

million tons were registered in the Port. But the silting which had been partly responsible for Chester's failure to become a major port, threatened the Mersey and a system of revetments or walls were built on both sides of the river to hold back the encroaching sand banks and maintain the channel.

In the first decade of the new century came further development. In 1907, the Dock Office - now the Port of Liverpool Building - was opened on the southern area of the filled-in George's Dock. Parliamentary powers were obtained for a large extension of the dock system to the north of the Liverpool Dock Estate - through the

construction of the Gladstone Dock. However, owing to developments in shipbuilding, the Board first developed a graving dock - a dry dock from which water is excluded by means of gates after it has been drained, so that ships can be repaired - in advance of the main scheme. The Gladstone Graving Dock was opened by King George V on July 11th, 1913.

Within a week of the outbreak of World War 1, Princes Landing Stage was being used as an embarkation point for troops and horses for the British Expeditionary Force. The Government appointed a committee in the following year for the co-ordination of the naval, civil and military requirements of the port, and in 1916 a Port Labour Committee was set up to deal with exempting essential dock labourers from being called up. The exemption was later extended to many ancillary workers. Dockers were enlisted into a military wing usually known as the "Khaki Dockers".

The construction of the Gladstone wet docks had been interrupted by the outbreak of war but in July 1927 King George V made another visit to the Port for a formal opening of the entire Gladstone Dock System. After lunch at the Town Hall, their Majesties boarded the Mersey Docks and Harbour Board vessel Galatea at the Princes' Landing Stage and sailed down the river, entering the Gladstone Lock and breaking a ribbon that had been stretched across the entrance. At the east end of the Branch Dock the King declared the docks open with the

stirring words: "The increase of commerce is of far more than local interest. The expansion of your trade implies the advancement of world commerce." In the meantime, the first stage of electrifying the dock estate from Sandon to Hornby Docks was authorised in 1918 - the same year that 720,000 US and Canadian troops disembarked in Liverpool.

In June 1920 a coasting steamer, the Countess, carried away the inner gates of the 30ft lock of the Alfred river entrance at Birkenhead. In the resulting rush of water the Countess and several barges were swept into the river and many of them sank. It was another two years before work on the reconstruction of the Alfred river entrances was begun. With another war looming, a Port Emergency Committee was set up to ensure a quick turn-round of ships and clearance of cargoes. The first bombs of World War II fell on the docks in Birkenhead in August 1940 and bombs hit Brunswick Dock in Liverpool just a few days later. The most devastating year for the docks was 1941 when the Dock Office was hit, burning out the east block and the top floor. The following day the SS Malakand, carrying 1,000 tonnes of shells and bombs was berthed in Huskisson Dock when she was hit during a bombing raid, caught fire and exploded. Parts of the ship were found two and a half miles away. Liverpool became the focal point for the longest battle of the Second World War - the Battle of the Atlantic - as merchant ships ran the gauntlet of hunting U-boat packs to carry vital supplies from Canada and America to besieged Britain. At the Western

Approaches strategic centre close to Liverpool's Pier Head, the convoys and their protection by warship and aircraft were planned and their perilous passage plotted. During the war 75 million tonnes of cargo and 4.7 million troops passed through Liverpool. The Atlantis, the first ship carrying repatriates, arrived in October 1943 with 800 badly wounded servicemen from German prison camps. In the same year the Dock Board began building canteens on the docks. By the end of the war, there were 57 of them with seating for 13,600 and serving 90,000 meals a day.

In 1946 work was started on the Riverside Station to carry passengers on trans-Atlantic and other liner services almost to the ship's side. Two years later Liverpool established the world's first port radar system for the control and safeguarding of shipping. With a 20 mile range, it was opened at the North West corner of Gladstone Dock.

In 1953 the Canadian Pacific liner Empress of Canada - one of many grand passenger ships sailing from Liverpool to North America and other parts of the world - was gutted by fire and capsized in Gladstone Dock. The wreck was

Left: An aerial view of the docks. In the age of general cargo as many as 100 ships could be in port on any one day. Below: The closing days of sail.

lifted the following year and sold for scrap. Three years later, in 1956, the overhead railway which had become known as the "dockers umbrella" was closed, its fate sealed after 63 years by the affect of the destructive industrial atmosphere and the weather upon its wrought-iron and steel structure. The port continued to be busy in the 1960s. Liverpool established another first by leading UK ports into the computer era. It was the first British port and only the fourth in the world to install a computer.

In 1964 a feasibility study was begun into a new deep water dock to the north of the Gladstone area to cater for larger ships and cargo volumes and in 1966 the plans were revised to allow for the rapid development in containerisation of cargo. The following year work was started on construction of the new dock. Meanwhile, container ships were accommodated from May 1967 at the Gladstone container berth, a facility created from the Gladstone graving dock. The end of the 1960s and early 1970s were years of financial crisis for the port which came as near to closure as at any time in its history. With a capital structure still largely based on concepts from when it was set up a century before, the Mersey Docks and Harbour Board struggled to adjust to technological change and adapt the port for the new era in shipping. With the Board unable to meet its debts, a bill was put before Parliament in 1970 to make the Port Authority a statutory company

and in 1971 the passing of the Mersey Docks and Harbour Act changed the former Board to The Mersey Docks and Harbour Company. At about the same time, the £50 million dock development at Seaforth - the largest and most costly development in the port's history - came on stream and was officially opened by HRH The Princess Anne as the Royal Seaforth Dock, the main features of which were a container terminal, grain terminal and forest products terminal.

It was in 1972 that the three miles of docks to the south of Liverpool's Pier Head were closed to shipping, their water too shallow and their narrow quays with dockside sheds no longer appropriate for modern shipping. The South Docks were acquired from Mersey Docks by the Government appointed Merseyside Development Corporation and redeveloped using taxpayers funds.

In the Port of Liverpool, positive developments at the beginning of the 1980s included the opening of a £950,000 Freightliner rail terminal at Royal Seaforth which has developed into a busy facility moving containers and steel to and from other regions of the UK. But by 1982 cargo through the Port of Liverpool had fallen to 9.3 million tonnes and Mersey Docks faced a £10 million deficit. The impact of containerisation and adverse changes in the structure of North West industry were compounded by Britain's entry into the Common Market which favoured South and East Coast ports. In addition, poor industrial relations in the docks throughout the late 1960s and 1970s drove away both shipping lines and shippers. This nadir in Liverpool's fortunes prompted the Mersey Docks and Harbour Company to implement a major rationalisation programme to bring the Port and its own interests back to good health. The changes involved large scale voluntary severance of surplus manpower, changes in working practices, many of which were secured in the first two-year pay deals negotiated in the British ports industry, and an entrepreneurial approach to development of the business.

In 1984 Mersey Docks made a profit of £800,000 on turnover of some £50 million. The Port handled little more than 9 million tonnes of cargo but that year was the turning point which marked the beginning of the renaissance of Liverpool as one of Britain's most successful ports. 1984 also marked the launch of Liverpool Freeport, Britain's largest and leading

free zone. Located on both banks of the Mersey, the Freeport has been a focal point for maritime regeneration initiatives by Mersey Docks working in partnership with Wirral and Sefton Borough Councils under the Government's City Challenge schemes. Throughout the second half of the 1980s and into the 1990s, the Mersey Docks and Harbour Company developed into a Group of related interests. In 1993 it acquired the Medway ports of Sheerness and Chatham in Kent and in 2001 bought the Lancashire port of Heysham. It owns the major container shipping line on the Irish Sea and operates terminals in Dublin, Belfast and Cardiff. The international arm of the Company is the largest port management consultancy in the UK and provides support and assistance to other ports throughout the world.

With the Port of Liverpool handling record volumes of cargo, Mersey Docks invested more than £50 million in expanding the Port and Freeport. Part of the historic Dock Road, for years the main artery between the city centre and the miles of berths which made Liverpool one of the world's great trading cities, was closed to public traffic - not as a reflection of decline but to allow the expansion of the Port by another 70 acres for development of nearly 1 million sq ft of additional warehousing.

Over several years from the turn of the new millennium, the Royal Seaforth Container Terminal underwent a £25 million refurbishment involving expansion of the container park, construction of new facilities, introduction of new ship-to-shore gantry cranes and other plant and the application of new computer systems to increase the efficiency of the operation. The Royal Seaforth Container

Liverpool double to around 40 a year.

In September 2005, the Mersey Docks and Harbour Company was acquired by Peel Ports Group, one of Britain's leading transport and property companies, with strong involvement in airport and seaport operations. The acquisition of Mersey Docks transformed Peel's Ports sector from a group handling 20 million tonnes of cargo a year into the UK's second largest port cluster handling 63 million tonnes of cargo a year. With over 33 million tonnes of freight a year moved through its docks, Liverpool represents more than 50% of Peel Ports Group's trade. The other ports in the sector are Clydeport in Scotland, the Lancashire Port of Heysham, the Manchester Ship Canal and Medway Ports in the South East of England.

Terminal, the UK's third largest container facility on volume and the country's major gateway for container trade with North America, handles more than 600,000 TEUs (Twenty Foot Equivalent Units) a year and serves over 50 global destinations. Another £25 million was invested in development of the Twelve Quays River Terminal at Birkenhead for Irish Sea roll-on roll-off ferries. Completed in 2002, the terminal is operated by Norfolk Line, a subsidiary of the world's largest shipping company, who have two sailings a day to both Belfast and Dublin, carrying large volumes of freight, passengers and their cars.

In response to growth in container trade and new influences upon the industry, the Port of Liverpool is planning the largest development since the Royal Seaforth Dock was built. A new £80 million river container terminal capable of simultaneously handling two of the new generation of post-Panamax size container ships, which are too large to enter the Port's established enclosed dock system, is planned for a site on the Mersey close to Seaforth and Gladstone Docks. There are also plans for an extension to Liverpool Landing Stage at Pier Head to create a cruise ship facility at which the largest cruise vessels can berth to allow their passengers to walk ashore. The Liverpool City Council initiative, with the support of Mersey Docks, is expected to be complete by Liverpool's year as European Capital of Culture in 2008. The development could see the number of cruise ships visiting

A chapter of the Port of Liverpool's long history is now being re-written. For the first time the Port is one with the Manchester Ship Canal. The 36 mile long waterway from Eastham Lock on the River Mersey to the heart of Greater Manchester, was built at the end of the 19th century by merchants determined to avoid having to pay the high price applied at that time, to moving cargo through the Port of Liverpool and on to Manchester by rail. Now, under the Peel Ports umbrella, the Port of Liverpool and the Ship Canal have become a single seaway for global freight, a water highway for the most diverse range of cargo and shipping, amounting to more than 40 million tonnes a year of international trade.

Left: A floating grain elevator discharging a ship at Liverpool. Above: In the days of steam most of Liverpool's docks were linked by rail. Right: A birds eye view of Royal Seaforth Dock under construction in 1972.

Robert Lunt & Sons - Firmly in the saddle since 1836

In 2006 one of Liverpool's most enduring family firms Robert Lunt & Sons Ltd, now based in Canal Street, Bootle, celebrated 170 years in business.

Today's Managing Director, Christopher Lunt, presides over a thriving company renowned for its product range of tarpaulins, cargo straps and banners supplied to the haulage industry - but it also has some rather more unexpected customers.

Company founder, the eponymous Robert Lunt, established the business in 1836 when he began producing top quality saddlery - principally for teams of heavy horses then used for pulling wagons with loads of cotton, rubber, wool, timber, tobacco, fruit, sugar etc...from the docks to massive warehouses, some 10 storeys high.

Arrival of the internal combustion engine and subsequent motor vehicles presented no immediate threat to the next generation.

The founder's son, another Robert, continued the business and at his death in 1903 was using premises now no longer in existence, at 53-59 Cranmer Street. The buildings there included a dwelling house, stables and a workshop. At the time of the younger Robert Lunt's death the business was also using premises at 71 Old Hall Street, which had been bought on a 75 year lease in 1900 for £800, at a time when mortgage rates were 5%. These premises were 5 storeys high on a corner site extending 40 ft down Brook Street.

Top left: Founder Robert Lunt.
Top right: Son of the founder Robert Lunt. **Right:** A letter of notification from Thomas Porter & Sons on the taking over of the firm by Robert Lunt & Sons.

Even by his death in 1903 the second Robert Lunt would have had little inkling of where the future lay. By then there were a few thousand motor vehicles on the roads but they were still vastly outnumbered by the millions of horses used for every purpose and the business of making heavy horse gears was as brisk as ever.

An interesting figure in the 1919 accounts states 1 horse and 2 traps at £70, with running costs of £119.19 shillings & 7 pence.

The founder's eldest grandson, Henry Christopher Lunt (1867-1941) continued the business from 71 Old Hall St, 7 Stanley Rd, Kirkdale and also 33 Gt Nelson St which was aquired after taking over another well established firm Thomas Porter& Sons in 1936. This enabled Lunts to extend their contacts morewidely in the S. W. Lancs agricultural community and increase the number and range of items stocked. Items such as binder canvasses and elevators began to be made for reaping machines. Unfortunately in the May Blitz of 1941 no 33 received a direct hit and the letter from the Board of Trade shows the sum of £ 1380.1.3. as being compensation for the total loss of building, fittings, and stock in trade.

From early on the firm had exhibited throughout the area and won prestigious medals for quality products. The stand at the Liverpool Show in the 1930s depicts the variety of stock items, members of the family and also Mr John William Murray who worked with the firm for nigh on 60 years.

The Old Hall Street site with the sloping Brook St provided a suitable well lit cellar working space and it was here that all the horse collars were made. Tom Banks, a wonderful craftsman, could make an entire heavy horse collar in slightly less than a day.

This was an amazingly skilful operation especially when one realises that his only instruction would be the depth of the collar, the width of the shoulders and whether the horse had a "narrow neck" or not. Horses which had agressive habits when their ears were touched had to have open top collars made.

thus forming a wide tube. By varying the amount of rye straw put into this tube and by varying the number and size of the looped stitches the shape and size of the collar gradually formed. When all the stuffing had been finished, two straps would be fixed for attaching to the saddle and the outer facing would be fixed too.

Everything was done by hand. The first thing made was a "pipe" of leather stuffed hard with rye straw cut to exact length; the pipe being closed as the stuffing took place. To this was attached strips of fine linen canvas lining on the inside of the pipe. The other side of the strip was attached to the outside edge of the pipe by large hand sewn loops of strong linen twine, back to the outside edge of the pipe,

Rye straw was particularly well suited to this job and the cool cellar provided ideal storage as it was only harvested once a year. A small patch of rye was grown especially for Robert Lunt by Cooks of Catchdale Moss near St Helens.

Other craftsmen shared a workshop on the first floor where, among others, Will Eaton made all of the cavalry style saddlery for the Liverpool Mounted Police as well as the Lancashire Constabulary; work was also done for the City of Edinburgh Force. All of this work was made using brown leather. Matt Lawless worked solely on "black work" making saddles, fitting the beautifully shaped flaps and pads onto the oak "tree" which determined the form of the saddle and also bore the galvanised crank which carried the ridgeworth (a twisted chain) over the shaft horse's back and linked up with the shafts on either side. From the back of the saddle the crouper ran along the horse's spine and ended in the dock which was located over the tail. Down from the crouper on the horse's flanks fell straps which were attached to the breechen. This was effectively the brakes of the wagon as it was a huge lined (two thicknesses) leather strap passing round the rump of the horse and again was linked to the shafts on either side.

Top: Medals awarded to Robert Lunt & Son, 1862 and 1883.
Left: Robert Lunt & Sons' five storeys high premises on the corner of Brook Street, mid 1920s.

Lunts were the only firm to make the renowned "cockleshell" blinkers fitted to their bridles. When relatively long runs of stitching had to be done a British United No 6 machine (pictured on page 98) was used. Lunts had two, one of which was heated by gas jets which played on various parts of the machine to ensure that the pitch black wax was molten when the thread was inserted into the leather.

Each craftsman had his own place, stool or "horse" clamp to hold the workpiece in position and his own

be "right" it would be waxed with beeswax and if yellow ready for immediate use. Similarly if the finished thread was to be white it would be waxed but if black it was drawn across black pitch wax before the beeswax was used. The beeswax provided lubrication as well as preservative qualities. Each thread thus

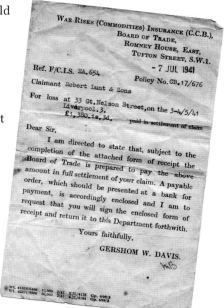

made was about 8 - 10 feet long and then had a needle fixed at each end thus making possible the figure of 8 stitches. On the edge of each man's bench a 30mm hole was drilled and filled with tallow. Usually he would dip each needle into this as well as the awl, a triangular shaped needle-like object mounted in a handle. The awl was thrust through the leather, held steady in the clamp, to make a hole through which the needles were passed in opposite directions and then pulled tight.

Making and maintaining regular sized and tensioned stitches was a highly skilled job and Williams was another person who excelled at this whatever article was being made, whether instrument cases, brief cases, veterinary surgeons' special appliances or even the occasional orthopaedic appliance.

The Cutting Room was also on the first floor and was where the selection of leather was made. Only three tools were used here, each hand held; a guage to check the thickness of the hide, the cutting guage and the round knife. Alongside the Cutting Room was a large slate tank of water which was used to soften leather

range of specialist tools. In those days each craftsman made his own thread according to what job was being done using different weights or strengths of hemp which would be either white or yellow. The strands of hemp would be passed over a hook fixed on the bench and the man would take a pace back then untwist the strand making it easy to break. Then holding both ends of the first strand he would step forward twice to make three ply or four times to make five ply. Next he would apply twist to the three or five strands by rolling it down a leather patch on his leg. When he judged it to

Above left: Robert Lunt Stands displaying a large selection of their stock at the Liverpool show in the 1930s pictured from left to right, John Murray who was with the firm for over 60 years, HC Lunt (jnr), HC Lunt (snr) and Mr RS Lunt. *Left:* Examples of old specialist tools and patterns used by craftsmen at Robert Lunt & Sons.
Above: A letter confirming settlement of compensation for bomb destruction during the second world war.

which had to be bent double before it was worked.

The whole first floor was heated by a large open fire in a black cast iron fireplace. The second floor used sewing machines for making horse cloths, nose bags and coal bags. The top floor was where tarpaulins were made using a twin needle sewing machine. When finished they would be stamped with the owner's name using stencils which hung round the walls.

At this time, entering from Old Hall Street, one walked past glass cases full of bridles, saddles, stirrups, bits, horse brasses, currycombs, whips and horsecloths. To the rear was the office, still with tall Dickensian writing desks lining the walls; very high chairs being needed to reach the writing slope. There was also a partners desk and an ancient intercom system which consisted of a speaking tube and whistle to attract the attention of the men on the upper floors. These fittings were still in use until the firm moved to Bootle in 1969, by which time however a telephone and typewriter had been added to them.

Many of the Team Owners (old speak for haulage contractor) had several hundred horses each, housed in yards, some half the size of a football pitch, with a midden in the middle. On each side were stalls, often for 30 or more horses. One notable yard had a two storey stable with a wooden ramp for the horses to use to reach their own stall at the end of the day. The Lunt children were sometimes taken to these when their father had to check collars for fitting or alterations.

Robert Slater Lunt (1901-1967) was the fourth generation to run the business. He became the family member who would witness great changes to the business during his lifetime with motor lorries superseding horse-drawn vehicles. Both he and his father were past Presidents of the National Association of Master Saddlers.

Farming requisites had always been part of the business. The Gt Nelson Street depot next to the wholesale fruit and vegetable market was used by farmers who sold their produce there and were then able to collect repaired harness and stock up on agricultural sundries such as spades, forks, rakes, boots, and galvanised goods such as buckets, incubators, and hoppers.

Gt Nelson Street was abandoned when the old fruit and vegetable market closed. The agricultural side of the business however survived and expanded. In the 1970s a bigger depot was bought at Rainford specialising in farm requisites such as pig, poultry and game rearing equipment. All types of wire, netting, field fencing, baler twine and ropes, paper packaging and veg nets together with a wide range of agricultural chemicals were sold. A further addition was NW Wilkinson Ltd of Banks near Southport: this depot specialised in goods for horticulture such as composts and chemicals. The agricultural side of the business was sold in the 1980s.

Lunt's was forced to leave Old Hall Street when the building was compulsorily purchased to make way for Liverpool's regeneration and moved to 9-23 Canal Street, Bootle, a few miles north along the dock road, where manufacturing continues.

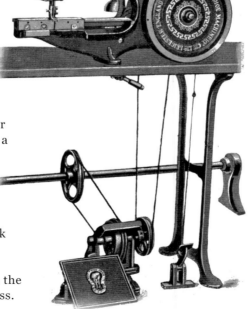

*Top: HC Lunt (left), third generation owner and RS Lunt fourth generation owner. **Left:** An early Saddlers' and Harness Makers' BU No6 machine.*

Today the premises in Canal Street no longer make saddlery. Horses have been superseded by motor lorries and trailers which require large curtains and tarpaulins. Large hatch covers for ships and awnings for sun decks on cruise liners plus various goods for the UK Atomic Energy Authority have been made since the move from Old Hall Street. More esoteric items manufactured now include specialist soft shelving for Jaguar's production lines and harnesses for the Euro Fighter's ejector seats. Special flexible containers are made to carry pharmaceuticals worldwide and safety devices have been designed & made for the newsprint industry.

Little hand-sewing remains today. Specialist Welding and machine stitching are now the norm. Computers for design and office work have replaced high desks and copperplate journals.

The current generation remembers many well known characters who have worked for the firm. Already mentioned are Tom Banks, Will Eaton, Matt Lawless, Ozzie Williams and John Murray but others too worked for many decades. Dunn and Tom Kempton from the 1920s onward and later Brenda Logan 18 years, Jack Smith 20 years, Eddy Kabluzenko 38 years and Derek Service 25 years and still in charge of production.

The current family member running the firm is Robert Christopher Lunt, the fifth generation. He also has witnessed and managed great changes; from shire horses to modern aircraft supplies.

According to a Liverpool Almanac of the 1880s ..."There is not an owner of rolling stock in the district to whom the firm is unknown: it is in the front rank of those of its kind".

Those standards have continued down to the present day and are seen in the company's accreditation to ISO 9002.

Top: Horses belonging to Thomas Wilson with saddlery manufactured by Robert Lunt & Sons Ltd. *Above left: Fifth generation of the family Mrs Margaret Swift, Mrs Jennifer Linstead and Robert Christopher Lunt current Directors of Robert Lunt & Sons Ltd.*

Blue Coat School - Learning history

Supposedly the best days of our lives, our school-days were certainly the longest since most of us could not wait for the bell to end each one of them!

Many of us stayed on at our local school only until the age of just 14 before leaving for the world of work. Other, somewhat younger, readers may have attended a 'Secondary Modern' or a brand new Comprehensive school. Still others may have passed their eleven-plus and gone to a Grammar school. And some will have attended a school which can trace its history across three centuries - Liverpool's Blue Coat School.

There are numerous Blue Coat Schools throughout the country. The oldest and most famous is Christ's Hospital school in the City of London (now relocated to Horsham, Surrey), which was founded in 1563.

Following the Reformation, when the monasteries were swept away, many public services such as health and

*Top: St George's Day celebrations outside Blue Coat Hospital, 1843. **Above right:** An early painting of Blue Coat by AR Cox.*

education, which until then had been provided by the church, also disappeared.

There was an urgent need for foundling hospitals, and in answer to that need Christ's Hospital in London was created - a place where poor children could be accommodated, cared for and taught. Blue is not a royal colour - that is purple, but it is the colour of alms giving and charity. It was a common colour for clothes in Tudor times and so the charity children were dressed in blue Tudor frock coats, yellow stockings and white neckbands at the throat. The children of the Liverpool Blue Coat School, both boys and girls would wear a distinctive, and archaic, uniform until 1948 when the 'Hospital' became a day and boarding school for boys.

Liverpool's Blue Coat Hospital was founded in 1708 by local merchant Bryan Blundell and by the school's first headmaster, the Reverend Robert Stythe, to teach poor children how 'to read, write and cast accounts'.

Blundell was a master mariner and part or sole owner of the ship Mulberry then engaged in 'the foreign trade'. Robert Stythe was the first joint Rector of Liverpool.

At that time there was no welfare state, but the great merchants in the area had a social conscience, and the foundation rapidly grew as an orphanage for Liverpool boys and girls.

The original building was located at Blue Coat Chambers in School Lane, on land which had earlier been occupied by Cross' Free Grammar School. The land on which the school was built - then part of the waste near St Peter's churchyard - was granted by the Corporation, and it was from this small school, built at a cost of just £35, that what was previously New Street took its new name - School Lane. Some 50 children were clothed and taught by the charity at this new day school, but fed and housed outside.

Out of school hours however children were apt to get into bad habits and Bryan Blundell therefore determined to change the school into one which took boarders; he immediately subscribed £750 with the promise of more, to improve the school. In 1719 the foundation stones of fine new buildings were laid; built in the Queen Anne style the buildings still function today as the Bluecoat Arts Centre. Building continued until 1725 by which time the total cost had amounted to £2,288 - almost all raised by donations.

Pupil numbers remained at about 50, made up of both boys and girls. By the closing years of the 18th century however numbers had risen to 375 boarders, many of whom were required to contribute to the school's coffers and earn their keep by working at spinning or pin-making.

Undoubtedly life was quite tough for those early pupils, though some were prepared to rebel: on 25th July 1800 for example no fewer than 107 of the boys escaped for the day to visit Liverpool Fair after they had removed a door catch.

In 1899 two of the Trustees placed at the disposal of the Hospital a site of seven and a half acres on the edge of Wavertree Playground. Some £80,000 was still needed for a new school building however, but one of the Trustees, WH Shirley, left the whole of his estate of £38,000 to the

Below: *Blue Coat Band circa 1910*

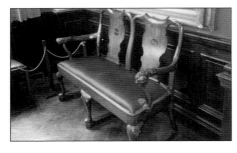

school and this, together with other gifts, enabled the work to proceed - as a result the school assembly hall is named the Shirley Hall in honour of the benefactor. The new building was designed by Messrs Briggs, FB Hobbs and Arnold Thornley in the late English Renaissance style: it was built by Morrison & Sons of Liverpool. Then in 1908, in its bicentennial year, the whole school moved to new premises in what was then the quiet village of Wavertree. The area still retains a village atmosphere with its coaching inns, green and lock-up.

One of the greatest treasures of the school is its chapel. The beautiful Fenwick-Harrison Memorial Chapel was built in the early years of the 20th century by T Fenwick-Harrison as a memorial to his late wife. The chapel remains in daily use for morning assembly. The faces of stone cherubs look down from its walls - each one different and carved by Edward O Griffin, a Liverpool sculptor and architectural carver.

The chapel was built from designs of the same architects who were responsible for the school building. The style is the late English Renaissance and is octagonal in form with a circular dome and transepts on three sides. The internal fittings are all oak, the walls being lined with Bath stone. The Chapel can accommodate about 500 people and was dedicated by the Lord Bishop of Liverpool in 1906.

Yet another 'treasure' is the Board Room which belongs to the Foundation Trustees and is used for Governors' meetings and special occasions. In the Board Room one will find a number of historic paintings - some by an old boy, Richard Ansdell RA.

Top left: *A very old and very valuable Treasurers seat, dating from the eighteenth century today has pride of place in the school boardroom.* **Below:** *Blue Coat Brotherly Society Triennial Treat, 1926.* **Right:** *The School's first XI cricket team of 1950.*

The school has remained in Wavertree since 1908, except for the period of the second world war: then the school, with its 270 boys and girls was evacuated to Beaumaris in Anglesey, North Wales where it remained until 1947.

In June 1940 the school buildings were requisitioned by the War Office and arrangements made for pupils, staff and furniture to be taken to Anglesey. By then, due to conscription, the male staff was reduced to the Headmaster, Senior Master and one assistant master: Mistresses were appointed to fill the vacancies.

At first pupils were taught in the Church Hall at Beaumaris and were billeted on the local community, but in 1941 the school rented Red Hill House from Sir Richard Bulkley where all the girls and a number of junior boys were installed. Later other temporary accommodation would be found, such as a house known as 'Bryn' and a disused Wesleyan Chapel in Church Street. Finally a beautiful house 'Woodgarth', which lay alongside the Menai Straits, was bought by the Trustees at a very reasonable price from the executors of FF Tattersall a generous friend of the school.

In the meantime Liverpool was being attacked by German bombers. The school at Wavertree was struck by incendiary bombs in May 1941, one of which set fire to the laundry and caused considerable damage. But, though the buildings may have been saved, when the school returned to Wavertree it came back to a very different post-war situation than the one it had left.

In 1949 Liverpool Education Authority approached the Governors of the Hospital with proposals that the Hospital should become a two-form entry Voluntary-Aided school for boys with boarding provision for those who needed it.

Girls would no longer be part of the reformed school, and with them went the distinctive uniform which had been such a memorable part of the school: in its place arrived the more conventional blue blazer.

The Governors decided in 1959 to draw up a programme for additions and extensions to the school in order to bring it into line with modern educational requirements. That programme would be complete by 1964. As a result four new and very pleasant classrooms, four modern and exceptional well equipped laboratories, a spacious and well-stocked library, a music room with new furniture and a piano, a new asphalted yard, and perhaps the most popular addition of all, a new swimming pool were added to the facilities at the school. Nor was the Boarding House forgotten: the Governors at a cost of £14,000 constructed ten new studies in a separate building in the South Quadrangle. The luxurious studies were furnished as a result of the generous gift of £550 from the Old Blues; a tuck shop was also added to the amenities of the Boarding side.

During the years following the end of the second world war the Boarding House was full, mainly from service families, boys who needed boarding facilities due to home circumstances, local boys with parents working abroad, and a group from the Seaman's Orphanage which had closed. It was real communal living, with open dormitories and bathroom. Bathing had to be strictly controlled as hot water was limited, being provided by an antiquated coal-fired boiler which Lewis, an 80 year old ex-naval stoker, permanently fed in the boiler house. Happy days - even if discipline was strict and everyone was up by 6.45 am and in bed by 9.30pm: being seen outside school without one's cap was a punishable offence.

By 1967 the total number of boys in the school was 518, but this included only a very small sixth form. Peter Arnold-Craft was appointed Headmaster in 1968 and was instrumental in transforming the school into what it is today. His influence is still felt by the current staff. He replaced Mr GG Watcyn who had been headmaster for 23 years and a teacher at the school since its orphanage days.

the school received over seven million pounds from the New Deal for Schools initiative, with a further £1.2 million from the School Foundation to refurbish the building.

In recent times under the leadership of Sandy Tittershill, a teacher at the school since 1966, the Blue Coat School has regularly featured amongst the top schools in the country in the Government's performance tables. In 2002 the school embarked upon a massive multi-million pound building programme which included ten new science laboratories, a sports hall, music centre and a new dining hall. These were all developed on the site of the school playground and, at the same time, the old swimming pool was demolished. The south side of the school which contained the former boarding wing was sold to make way for the development of 45 luxury flats, and the rest of the old building was restored, including the old dining room which was converted into a modern library and resources area. Girls were admitted to Year 7 in September 2002 for the first time since 1949. Lord Derby officially opened the new school buildings in 2004.

Another major change took place in 1989 when, 40 years after they had been excluded, girls were readmitted to the school to study in the sixth form. By 1995 the school would have 787 boys and 73 girls.

In July 1990, by which time the number of boarders had fallen to 29, boys' boarding provision came to an end and the Governors proposed to the Department of Education that the school became a four-form entry.

September 1991 saw that proposal accepted, and 30 more boys entered 'Year seven' or the first form. To accommodate the increase in numbers a phased building expansion programme was put in place. The first phase saw the introduction of four new classrooms, two new laboratories and a new art room. Phase two, which began in 1993, saw the conversion of the former boarding wing into further classrooms and specialist teaching areas. Part of the improvements would be funded by the generous bequest of £159,000 from the estate of Mrs Doris Croston after whom the school library would be renamed.

Phase three which began in 1994 saw the creation of new laboratories and other improved facilities. In April 1998

Today the school is looking forward to 2008 when it will celebrate its three hundredth anniversary, an event which happily coincides with the City of Liverpool's European Capital of Culture Year. In order to mark this special anniversary the school has launched a Special Appeal to raise one million pounds by 31st December 2007, via which the school aims to build an all-weather sports pitch on the games field as well as develop a new sixth form study area within the East Wing.

Though buildings and staff have changed endlessly over the course of three centuries one thing however remains constant: a commitment to academic excellence underpinned by the school motto - Non sibi sed omnibus - Not for oneself but for all.

Left: Blue Coat boarders greet their grandparents, 1930s.
Above: A birds eye view of the school in the 1970s. On the left hand side stands the old gymnasium and squash courts and on the right stands the old swimming pool. Both were demolished to be replaced by the new building which doubled the size of the school.
Right: Headmaster Sandy Tittershill (centre) is presented with a cheque from the Board of Trustees.

Medicash - Not for profit but for health

The eight centuries since Liverpool's birth in 1207 have seen the rise of a city which at various times has been the 'capital of enterprise'; the 'capital of shipping'; the 'capital of pop music'; the 'capital of comedy'; and even the 'capital of football'.

The people of Liverpool have a great deal to be proud of - both past and present. One reason for citizens to take particular pride in their city is the way in which healthcare provision was provided in the long years before the NHS came into being.

Important institutions were established in Liverpool in Victorian times to help ensure the people of Liverpool were able to obtain the healthcare they needed. One such institution which has not merely survived, but

thrived, since the days it was founded in the 19th Century is Medicash, an organisation whose Chief Executive Bill Gaywood says is proud of Liverpool, proud of its place in the city and its history, and proud to be able to help cast some light on the memories which make up the backcloth to all our lives.

Today Medicash is a not-for-profit organisation still dedicated to improving the standards of healthcare offered to its 200,000 members throughout the UK.

Top: *The Royal Liverpool Infirmary, 1878.*
Below: *The late 1920s, a queue of convalescence applicants wait to see the Council's Medical Referee at Preesons Row.*

The world of healthcare in the mid 19th century however was enormously different to that of today.

How did people pay for healthcare before the free NHS? Friendly societies and similar non-profit organisations providing members with sickness and injury insurance have been governed by legislation in the United Kingdom for more than 200 years.

The first Friendly Society Act was introduced in 1793.

Throughout the nineteenth century a huge growth of friendly societies took place. At the beginning of the century there were about 7,000 societies in existence - and by its end 30,000.

In those days the voluntary hospital system - unique to the UK - was the focal point of health services. Initially legacies and large donations from the better-off had funded these charitable hospitals.

The first fund specifically for supporting voluntary hospitals was set up in Birmingham in 1858. A Hospital Sunday Fund was formed: churches and chapels celebrated Hospital Sunday and collections were allocated to the local voluntary hospitals. But it also became clear that ordinary citizens and working people could also make regular contributions to voluntary hospitals - and directly benefit from doing so.

In 1860 the larger hospitals in Liverpool began to suffer major financial difficulties: the Liverpool Royal Infirmary launched an appeal to counter its problems, with the prospect that some patient services would have to be withdrawn if help was not forthcoming.

The Northern and Southern Hospitals did

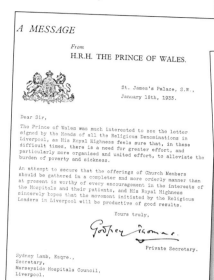

the same, and the people of Liverpool were tasked with finding a minimum of £8,000 to help. The appeals struck a chord in the city and brought an immediate response which meant that the crisis was temporarily averted.

The lesson that was learned from the appeals was that regular weekly contributions would be more effective than going cap-in-hand each time a crisis loomed - and that was the idea behind the establishment of the Hospital Saturday Fund in the 1871. By 1890 a committee had been set up: it was composed of elected employees of subscribing firms, with a full time paid secretary, and organised weekly collections.

Such weekly contributions under these health cash plans proved popular, and the numbers of people taking part grew quickly since contributors became eligible to obtain hospital treatment without further charge.

By 1894 the movement was turning into a major influence on health provision, with Fund representatives appointed to the boards of management of new hospitals, and a

Above left: A letter from HRH The Prince of Wales giving his support to the efforts of Liverpool's religious leaders and their attempts to alleviate the burden of sickness and poverty in the city, 1933. **Above right:** A letter received from the Rt Hon. Earl of Derby supporting the Merseyside Voluntary Hospitals, 1928. **Left:** The Merseyside Health Benefits Council's Penny in The Pound Fund contribute to a new Ambulance for Age Concern.

ladies' committee established, so that women could help with the fundraising.

Meanwhile the National Health Insurance Act of 1911 marked the beginning of a new phase in the role of friendly societies.

The Act required compulsory contributions from employees and employers in return for benefits such as the services of a GP. It was the first piece of legislation which applied insurance principles to healthcare and unemployment benefit. The 1911 National Health Insurance Act, marked a significant and fundamental change in the method of financing universal welfare, made possible only by the long and painful experience by friendly societies. The task of administering the scheme fell to them.

Voluntary benefits were secured from societies as previously but separate management and resources were made available to administer the state scheme. These functions were authorised by the government and their expenses met. Such sections within existing societies were known as 'Approved Societies'. Thus began an extraordinary partnership, set to last until the introduction of the welfare state in 1948.

From 1910 to 1947, friendly societies administered the state sickness benefit scheme and, at their peak in 1945, also catered for the further needs of 8.75 million private subscribers through over 18,000 branches or societies.

Meanwhile in Liverpool fundraising was so successful that by 1918 the Hospital Saturday Fund receipts were £10,000-plus and rising.

Then, as now, however the costs of providing healthcare grew to outstrip funding and the 1920s saw a shortfall in income: further action was required.

In an attempt to find a solution to the recurring problem, in 1927 a wider-ranging organisation was set up - the Merseyside Voluntary Hospitals Contribution Fund. This soon became known as the Penny in the Pound Fund because each contributor was asked to give a penny from each pound he earned (as long as he was in a job and in good health).

The contributors' employers were asked to add to the amount given by their workers, with the result that the voluntary hospitals were able to rely on a stable annual income, with contributing workers entitled to free treatment.

The funding meant that services were able to develop, with an ambulance service started in 1929, at around the same time as a convalescence and after-care service.

In 1931 the official title became the Merseyside Hospitals Council, an indication of how closely the Fund had become identified with the hospitals.

The Council's work continued and increased during the war years of 1939 to 1945 with its

Top: Southport Hospital receives the key to a new coach from representatives from the Merseyside Hospitals Council. *Left:* The Rt Hon. Kenneth Robinson Minister for Health opens the Mary Bamber Convalescent Home, May 1968.

After 1948 some 200 of the 235 'Hospital Cash Plan' organisations closed down: the remainder reinvented themselves. The big difference now was that most of the contributions could be returned to the contributors as benefits.

This was a fundamental change and meant that benefits, which at first were limited to inpatient stays in hospital, diversified so that they could be classed as Health Benefits rather than Hospital Benefits.

It also meant that the geographical area covered by the scheme extended. Instead of operating mainly in the Merseyside area, it covered the entire province of the Liverpool Regional Hospital Board, including Wrexham and the Flintshire coast, Chester, Warrington, St Helens and Southport. In time, Skelmersdale and Winsford were also brought in.

affairs administered by a War Emergency Committee under its chairman W Sutcliffe Rhodes. As well as maintaining its existing services, the Council also helped the war effort: it assisted the Civil Defence Emergency Committee whilst the Secretary, Sidney Lamb, organised the Lord Mayor's Liverpool War Fund Appeal.

This appeal provided comforts and amenities for members of the forces in the city.

During the war contributors were asked to pay an extra penny a week: half of the additional funds went to the hospitals and half to the Merseyside Civic Authorities for War Relief. Their extra contributions meant that around £115,000 was distributed to civic war charities.

The National Health Service was set up in 1948, with resulting effects on the activities of the organisation. While most of the financial burden had transferred to the new NHS, the Fund still had a major role to play in providing all kinds of services.

The start of the NHS had seen the end of the organised Hospital Sunday Services, which had been held every year since 1870 and raised £505,789 for distribution to the Merseyside voluntary hospitals.

The Fund's status as a charity was challenged in the 1960s by the Board of Trade, which claimed that the payment of benefits to contributors was in essence a business arrangement. This challenge resulted in an Emergency General Meeting of the Council in December 1968 deleting the 'charitable' clause from its constitution.

*Top left and above left: The Lord Mayor visits Liverpool Royal Infirmary, Christmas 1974. **Below:** The opening of a Hospital Shop by means of a grant provided by the Merseyside Health Benefits Council's Penny in the Pound Fund.*

That meant that the Penny in the Pound Fund could no longer operate as a charity, although the Council continued to act as trustee of the charitable funds under a scheme approved by the Charity Commissioners. These funds paid for all kinds of amenities for hospitals, children's and old people's homes, hostels and so on.

In 1974 - for the first but far from the last time - the NHS was reorganised, with Health Authorities and Family Practitioner Committees taking the place in the NHS system of hospitals management committees, local authorities and NHS executive councils. This reorganisation, coinciding with the establishment of Merseyside County Council and local authority boundary changes, provided the opportunity for the Merseyside Hospitals Council to reconsider its own name and constitution.

Taking advantage of this opportunity, the Council decided to keep the popular asset of the Penny in the Pound Fund name, while changing the Council's own name to Merseyside Health Benefits Council. The new name better reflected the purpose of the Council, whilst the Penny in the Pound name was still important to loyal customers.

Another change at this time of reorganisation was to appoint a new president of the Council. For years, the Lord Mayor of Liverpool had held this office, but the Lord Lieutenant of Merseyside, Sir Douglas Crawford, was now approached, and in April 1974 his first official function was to preside over the Annual General Meeting at Liverpool Town Hall.

The 1970s were hard times for Merseyside, with high unemployment and numbers of companies cutting workforces, or even ceasing to exist. Contributor numbers dropped by 12,750, and the remaining contributors agreed to increase their contributions - with the result that

Top: Children having fun at Olive Mount Children's Hospice. **Above:** *Mossley Hill Hospice.*

reserves remained more than adequate to satisfy the Insurance Companies Acts.

After 46 years in offices in Lord Street, the Council moved to new premises in Sir Thomas Street, in 1976. The new offices allowed all contributors' facilities to be housed on the ground floor.

For more than 20 years, these offices were the home - in customers' eyes - of the Penny in the Pound Fund. But the pace of change was accelerating, as the health insurance market became increasingly sophisticated, and the old model of a single contribution rate became outdated.

Even though the Penny in the Pound name still generates widespread recognition and goodwill on Merseyside it was under a new banner - Medicash - that major reforms began in the 1990s, reforms which are continuing to this day.

A number of new products were designed to meet the needs of the changing market, and to recognise the changing pattern of treatment within the NHS. At the same time recognising that there were opportunities for growth beyond Merseyside: it is now one of the top five firms in the industry, with an annual turnover around £27m, and reserves to match.

More than 200,000 customers across the UK enjoy the benefits of Medicash membership, with growing numbers of corporate customers recognising the impact Medicash products can have on staff well-being.

Changes around the start of the 21st century - including moving back to Lord Street, to large offices in Merchants Court - meant the introduction of a national sales force, and a restructuring of the Executive Committee to a more modern Board of Directors.

But even as wide-ranging change continues, the traditional values remain, with an emphasis on prompt payment of claims and a recognition that all members are equally valuable to the success of the company.

There is also a deep commitment to supporting the NHS through grants to help provide amenities that could not otherwise be financed. In 2006, more than £200,000 was committed for that purpose. So, even 135 years after the fund was first established to support voluntary hospitals - and even though today's financial figures would have been staggering to the pioneers of 1871 - the organisation's founding principles remain the same.

When people talk about Liverpool in these opening years of the new century, the conversation is all about progress, redevelopment and major schemes which are changing the face of the city. And while this is a great time to be a Liverpudlian, with 21st century excitement all around, it shouldn't be forgotten that the city has, thanks to organisations such as Medicash and its predecessors, already been a great place to live for a very long time indeed.

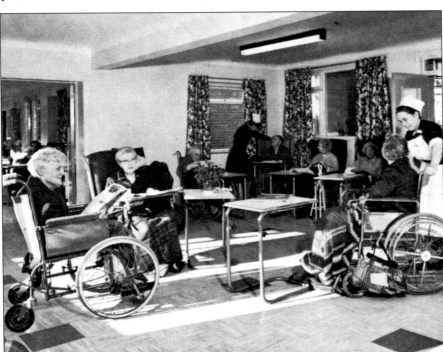

Top: Merseyside Health Benefits Council, Sir Thomas Street, Liverpool.
Left: Brandreth Hospice, Ormskirk.

Merseytravel - Ferries across the Mersey - and tunnels, trains and buses too!

Ferries: Monks at a Priory in Birkenhead began operating a ferry across the Mersey in 1330. The Merseyside Passenger Transport Authority and Executive have been responsible for the area's ferry train and bus services since 1969, and its tunnels since 1986. In 1987 they adopted the trading name of Merseytravel.

Liverpool Town Council began running its own ferry in 1840. The Wallasey and Birkenhead Corporations followed suit.

During both the first and second world wars several Wallasey ferries were conscripted for active service.

By the end of the second world war the fleets were aging, and during the 1950s new ferries were acquired. In 1951 the first world war veteran Royal Iris was renamed St Hilary in order to make way for the arrival of the new twin-screw diesel electric Royal Iris. The Leasowe was also added to the fleet that year, followed by Egremont in 1952 and the Royal Daffodil II in 1958. In 1960 the Woodchurch arrived and in 1961 the Mountwood replaced the Claughton, the last steam ferry. A year later the fleet was

added to by the Overchurch, the first all-welded construction ferry on the Mersey. In 1963 the very last steam powered ferry service was run to help out with the Whitsuntide rush.

In 1968 the ferry services were merged under the Merseyside Passenger Transport Executive and Mersey Ferries

Above: *Pictured during the second world war. At this time all ferries and luggage boats (top) were required to contribute to the war effort.*

was born. The Merseyside Passenger Transport Authority and Executive became operational a year later and took control of all the Municipal Transport undertakings of Liverpool, Birkenhead and Wallasey. During the 1970s the last New Brighton ferry sailed, the Egremont, was withdrawn and the Royal Daffodil II left the Mersey for the Mediterranean. The Royal Iris on the other hand helped launch the career of the Beatles, the Searchers, and Gerry and the Pacemakers as well as carrying distinguished passengers such as the Queen and Prince Phillip. In 1985 she set off on a Merseyside publicity cruise round Lands End up the River Thames and to Tower Bridge before conducting her last cruise in 1991.

By the mid-1980s commuter passenger numbers had declined and consequently in 1989 a total of £5 million was invested to re-launch the operation as a heritage and visitor attraction. The Heritage cruises proved to be a hit: the terminals were improved with added archive and history panels, gift shops, cafes and, at the Seacombe terminal, an aquarium displaying marine life found in the Mersey. In 1998 Overchurch was refurbished and renamed the Royal Daffodil. In 2002 Mountwood was renamed Royal Iris of the Mersey. The

Woodchurch became the Snowdrop in 2004. Equally significantly the £10 million 'Spaceport' opened at Mersey Ferries Seacombe terminal in 2005 with more investment planned.

Trains
Launched in 1866 the Mersey Pneumatic Railway project was unfortunately abandoned as sufficient funds could not be raised. In 1880 however Major Samuel Isaac met the entire cost of opening a railway under the Mersey.

In 1881 construction of the tunnel got under way with a toast from the Mayors of Liverpool and Birkenhead. The Mersey Railway was opened on 20th January 1887 by HRH the Prince of Wales and in celebration the city's banks closed between 11.30am and 2.30 pm whilst the church bells rang out across the city. Despite its promising start the early optimism proved unfounded: two years later the Mersey Railway was bankrupt. In 1893 the competing Liverpool Overhead Railway, nicknamed

Top: 'Snowdrop', one of the current fleet of Mersey Ferries.
Left: One of the original Westinghouse 'Chicago Style' electrics that replaced the steam stock in May 1903.

the Dockers Umbrella because the dockworkers sheltered under it, was opened. This was the only elevated railway in Britain and the first electric railway in the world.

By 1900 the Mersey Railway passenger numbers had gone down from 10 million to 8.5 million and the first class rolling stock was no longer maintained. The grime and smoke deterred passengers from using the trains in hot weather and the company also lost many of its passengers to the ferries. In 1902 the company could not even cover its expenses and its future was in question. The answer came with electrification, which was brought to the company by George Westinghouse. George owned the British Westinghouse Electric and Manufacturing Company and after coming into contact with Mersey Railway whilst looking for orders he decided to fund the venture himself to the tune of £3 million and guarantee an electrified system would be in operation within 18 months. The electrification was completed in 1903 and the stations and tunnels were cleaned and fitted with electric lighting. The future of the Railway was secured.

Throughout the 1930s the system was enhanced with the electrification of the Wirral section of the LMS company, and in 1936 six-car trains were introduced in the company's maroon and white livery in order to cope with the increase in passengers. The post-war period was marked by nationalisation; Mersey Railway was incorporated into the London Midland region of British Railways. It soon became evident that public transport needed to be improved in order to avoid congestion on the roads. This improvement was achieved in 1962 when proposals were put forward to convert the separate lines and terminals into an integrated system. The Mersey Railways Extension Act received Royal Assent in 1968 and the Mersey Railway was extended to form a loop underneath Liverpool City centre connecting all four existing routes. A new link was completed connecting the Southport and Ormskirk lines to Liverpool Central and the electrification was extended southwards and northwards. The work was finally completed in 1978 and the Merseyrail Underground was opened by the Queen.

During the 1980s Merseyrail extended the electrification to Hunts Cross, Rock Ferry and Hooton; in 1985 over 50,000 people used the train to reach the centre of Liverpool. A year later that success was furthered when bus deregulation served to emphasise the reliable and fast Merseyrail system and resulted in passenger numbers rising by more than 12 per cent. Today the Merseyrail system comprises three closely linked lines: the electrified Wirral, Northern Line and City Lines. With over 34 million passengers using the trains every year Merseytravel is set to continue expanding and improving rail services for many years to come, not least with major rolling stock refurbishments in partnership with Serco/Nedrail costing £32 million, and Liverpool South Parkway station providing links to the south of the city, to regional rail services, and the expanding John Lennon Airport.

Above: *Liverpool Central High Level Station pictured at the turn of the 1970s.*

Tunnels

The Mersey Ferries and the Mersey Railway had coped admirably with the transportation of passengers from the Wirral to Liverpool, but the cross-river transportation of road vehicles presented another challenge. The ferries had coped with the early motor traffic but by the 1920s the volume of vehicles had dramatically increased and was growing.

In 1825 the problem had actually been recognised, when the construction of an under-river road tunnel had first been proposed. The advent of the railway led to the idea being shelved for almost a century. Liverpool City hosted an inaugural meeting of neighbouring towns to propose the building and financing of either a tunnel or a bridge to improve traffic flow across the Mersey in 1914.

The outbreak of war however halted further progress until 1920 when the 'Cross River Traffic Committee' was resurrected and the next year renamed 'Merseyside Municipal Co-coordinating Committee' chaired by Sir Archibald Salvidge.

The resulting report advised against the construction of a bridge since in the event of another war its destruction could close the port of Liverpool. Instead the report supported the construction of a tunnel. On 8th August 1925 Royal Assent was given to Private Bill authorising the project under the guidance of the newly established Mersey Tunnel Joint Committee.

On 16th December 1925, at the bottom of the dry and disused Georges Dock, Princess Mary (later the Princess Royal) turned a golden key to start the boring machine which began work on the new tunnel.

The tunnelling work was carried out from both sides of the river. In 1928 the final breakthrough was made by Sir Archibald Salvidge, followed by the shaking of hands through the hole between the Lord Mayor of Liverpool and the Mayor of Birkenhead.

After the excavation of 1,200,000 tons of rock and gravel and the expenditure of £8 million the Queensway Tunnel was opened by King George V on 18th July 1934. Almost 80,000 people walked through the tunnel – the sixpence each paid for the privilege going to charity.

At its opening motor vehicles were not the only things expected to use the tunnel: tolls were also set for flocks of sheep, herds of cattle, pigs, horses, wagons, handcarts, wheelbarrows and wheelchairs!

Left and below: The building of the Mersey Tunnel in 1927.

excavated using a giant mechanical 'mole' manufactured in the USA. The result was twin tube tunnel, each tube with two traffic lanes twelve feet wide and just under two miles long. The ambitious project was opened by Queen Elizabeth II in June 1971.

In recent years considerable investment has been made in modern safety related improvements, such as escape refuges and cross tunnels to meet with current safety standards. Today the Mersey Tunnels continue to play a major role in the Merseyside transport network and work alongside the Mersey Ferries and Merseyrail.

Buses

In 1898 electric trams were introduced to Merseyside, the first tram running from South Castle Street to Dingle. In 1903 the whole system was converted to electrical power. Over the following years the tram system developed into one of the largest systems in the country, and was renowned for the amount of reserved track it had in use which it reserved to speed up journey times. Throughout the 1930s Merseyside's tramways were progressively abandoned and replaced by motorbuses. The conversion from tram to bus was completed in the 1950s.

Following the end of the second world war there was a boom in motoring. In 1965 Royal Assent was given for the Mersey Tunnel Joint Committee to finance and build a second tunnel and in 1966 work began on the Wallasey Tunnel —later to be renamed Kingsway. Sandstone was

Above: The Lord Mayor of Liverpool, Miss Margaret Bevan, and the Mayor of Birkenhead, Alderman F Naylor, shake hands through the hole in the dividing rock, 1928.
Below: A Green Goddess, one of Liverpool's famous streamlined trams.

increases, unemployment and a rise in car ownership. In an attempt to resolve the problem fares were reduced and this, combined with a successful marketing campaign, raised the number of passengers again.

The Local Government Act of 1985 decreed that the Passenger Transport Authority was to be made up of District Council representatives. A year later the transport Act brought far-reaching changes: any bus operator could run any service and charge any fare without subsidy; the Passenger transport Authority and Executive would have no control over commercial bus services. As a result the Executive's bus operations were transferred to a private company. Merseytravel however continues to provide high quality bus passenger facilities; not least Merseyside's modern bus stations, the most recent opening 2005 as part of Liverpool centre's massive Paradise Project.

The Merseyside Passenger Transport Authority and Executive - trading as Merseytravel – was formed to look after all aspects of transport in Merseyside. Today it is carrying forward that mission, through, under and around the River Mersey. Mersey Ferries, Merseyrail, Mersey Tunnels and the bus services are continuing the proud tradition of first-rate travel which began back in the 14th century.

From then on buses have provided Liverpool and surrounding areas with public transport on the roads and worked alongside the ferries and railways. In 1969 the Passenger Transport Authority and Executive took over responsibility for bus services with a remit to 'secure the provision of a properly integrated and efficient system of pubic passenger transport to meet the needs of the area'. In 1974 the work continued with the Merseyside County Council in its statutory role as Passenger Transport Authority.

At the time that the responsibility for bus services was taken over there were a total of five separate municipal bus operators in Merseyside, in addition to services provided by Ribble, Crossville and Greater Manchester. These services ran to different conditions and in many cases ran in wasteful competition with each other and with local rail services.

The Authority and Executive set to work developing changes to those outdated patterns and to improve the service to passengers. In order to improve co-ordination all picking up and setting down restrictions were removed, timetables were co-ordinated and wherever possible routes were combined. An improved bus service was implemented to reach the suburbs, and the trunk bus service reduced. New services were introduced to new housing areas that were previously neglected, and a Merseyside dial-a-ride bus service for disabled people and those unable to use conventional transport was implemented. These improvements were compounded with a substantial investment in bus operations: the entire fleet was replaced and improvements made to garages at Southport and St Helens.

Despite those vast improvements by 1981 there was a marked decline in the number of passengers due to fare

Top left: Bickerstaffe Street bus station in St Helens.
Below: The new Paradise Street interchange.

TJ Hughes - The first name in shopping

TJ Hughes is the best known name in London Road. The company is one of the most famous retailers in Liverpool, and a major name throughout England, Scotland and Wales.

From the day he was born on 21st March 1888 it was inevitable that founder Thomas J Hughes would some day become a retailer in his hometown of Liverpool.

Thomas' father James Hughes hailed from North Wales and was in the retail business. Young Thomas, a Welsh Liverpudlian, grew up surrounded by all aspects of trade.

The business dynasty began when James married his wife Anne. James had worked for Edward Morris and Anne too had gained vital experience working in a shop. In 1889 the couple bought their own shop in County Road, Walton.

Thomas would enjoy a childhood filled with memorable experiences of life in the retail trade. After leaving school Thomas served his apprenticeship as a draper at Audley House, then owned by Owen Owen.

On completing his apprenticeship Thomas worked briefly at Blackler's in Liverpool and then moved to London to work. After this work experience outside the family business Thomas moved back to Liverpool to work for his father. Thomas had clear ideas of how a business should be run, and was ambitious and innovative. Inevitably he and his father clashed. In October 1912 Thomas left his father's firm to set up his own business. Using his savings of £150, Thomas opened a shop at the corner of London Road and Norton Street with the name TJ Hughes above it. Despite its small size the business began to thrive. Thomas found that even a small concern with low profit margins could prosper given a high turnover.

The outbreak of the first world war brought with it a major disturbance. Thomas temporarily left the business to join the Royal Flying Corps. By that time Thomas was employing three assistants: whilst he was away he left the business in the capable hands of Miss Harris.

*Top left: Founder TJ Hughes. **Below:** An early line drawing depicting the shop in the 1920s. **Top Right:** Mr & Mrs Hughes join staff for an outing by steamer to Llandudno.*

TJ Hughes was ready to resume full trade at the end of hostilities in 1918. By then there was an addition to the Hughes' business in the shape of the first Babyland shop which had been opened in County Road by Mrs W Hughes in 1916.

Thomas' father James Hughes died in 1922. On James' death Thomas' brothers James and Hugh became partners in the firm that Thomas had quit ten years earlier. TJ Hughes flourished, but 1927 marked a turning point: Duncan Norman the managing director of Owen & Owen owners of Audley House was experiencing difficulties. One of the most urgent problems facing him was what to do with Audley House. The fine building, modelled on that of Marshal & Snelgrove in London's Oxford Street, was valued at £194,000. Now it was lying idle and its value had plummeted – at one point it was nearly sold for a mere £60,000.

Duncan decided to contact another draper in the London Road area: Thomas J Hughes. Thomas' business was thriving: he was employing 200 people and finding it difficult to cope with the ever-increasing business. The meeting with Duncan Norman could not have come at a better time. The two men agreed that Thomas would sell his business to a small private company to be known as TJ Hughes & Co Ltd. Thomas would become the sole managing director of the company with Duncan as the chairman and only other director. The newly-formed company would move into part of Audley House, with an option to expand. Thomas retained all the company's six per cent preference shares, and half the ordinary shares: the remainder being held by Duncan as nominee of Owen Owen Ltd. On 7th October 1927 the reconstituted company opened for business.

It was at Audley House that Thomas J Hughes began to gain a reputation for himself. Thomas was known by everyone who met him as a kindly man; well liked by everyone who knew him and with a genius for the drapery trade. One former staff member would recall being sent to the dentist to have her tooth extracted at her employer's expense, and then on another occasion being told by Thomas to take the day off when she was feeling ill and to go on an all expenses paid trip to Llandudno with her fiancé in order to recuperate.

Thomas got on well with Duncan Norman and would spend an hour or so each day discussing plans with him. On winter Saturdays, whenever Liverpool Football Club was playing at home, Thomas and Duncan would meet in the city and then walk all the way to Anfield to watch the game from a vantage point immediately behind the goalkeeper. Though not particularly interested in football himself Thomas went to the matches partly because he admired Liverpool's full back 'Parson' Jackson for the moral example he set the rest of the team.

Thomas was a tall man with a habit of rubbing his hands together when he was pleased. He was an acute observer, and much of his success stemmed from his ability to discover exactly what his customers most wanted and then provide it more cheaply than his competitors. Every morning he would walk past the other large drapery stores and note which were their most popular lines. On reaching Audley House he would present the list to his staff asking them to display the same lines prominently at a lower price. Thomas' motto was 'Buy dear and sell cheap' an apparently paradoxical inversion of common business sense, but a philosophy which Thomas made to work.

This however was not Thomas' only talent. Although his buyers carried out preliminary negotiations Thomas made all the final decisions himself, and even drafted his own advertisements for insertion in the Liverpool Echo. He also had a natural flair for fashion, and as a result had one of the most attractive shops in Liverpool. Success did not come without hard work and dedication and it was rare that Thomas took a holiday, even when he did he never forgot to telephone his assistants to find out what was happening.

The years following the move to Audley House were ones of unbroken prosperity. It was not long before TJ Hughes & Co Ltd took over the whole building.

Thomas' accounting system and some of his organisation was a little primitive, but because people flocked to see the

On 19th February 1932 Thomas J Hughes retired. His shares were bought at par for £35,000 by Owen & Owen Ltd. Sadly only a year after his retirement, on 14th April 1933, Thomas died in tragic circumstances, aged just 43.

Though the company still bore Thomas' name his death marked the end of an era. In the year of his death an advertisement was produced for the company announcing its '21 Years Progress'. The advert stated 'From a tiny shop with three assistants to the present huge store with a separate 'Household' building connected by subway. Such progress has not been equalled by any other retail store in the North of England!'

That progress could not have been achieved without Thomas' work, innovation and inspiration. Yet despite Thomas' departure the foundations had been laid for a consistently successful business.

By this time the company had begun conducting promotions outside Audley House and elsewhere. An advert from 1935 shows the promotion of 'Second and Final Week of Furniture Bargains At the Grosvenor Hotel Rhyl Organised by TJ Hughes & Co Ltd' at which all kinds of furniture was on offer, and, as the advertisement boasts, all the assistants spoke both Welsh and English.

Another promotion from this time was the holding of a 'Crooning & Talent Competition' organised by the company in conjunction with Gaumont British. To enter the competition candidates had to make a 6d (2 1/2p) record at the TJ Hughes recording studio of 'singing, crooning, reciting, mimicking, violin or piano'. The winner was sent on a 'free trip to London with a friend – all expenses paid, to visit Gaumont British Studio at Shepherd's Bush'.

bargains on offer turnover was enormous. One customer recalls buying a bed for 19s 11 d, (99p) two cups and saucers and plates for 1s 6d (7 1/2p) and a set of curtain material at 1s (5p) a yard – with bargains like those there is no wonder that Thomas was regarded as the pioneer of the cut price trade.

Inevitably after years of almost superhuman work Thomas began to feel the strain. Not least without a modern book keeping system he faced the formidable task of trying to keep track of everything single-handedly. Consequently Thomas' health began to suffer. Duncan tried to no avail to persuade him to take a holiday, and although there was nothing seriously wrong with him Thomas became convinced that he had contracted an incurable illness.

Top left: A spectacular 1950s view of TJ Hughes.
Top right: A staff picnic to Chester, 1928.

The outbreak of the second world war in 1939 saw TJ Hughes having to adapt to the changes brought about by the hostilities.

It was during the war that one of TJ Hughes' most inventive window displays was produced. The window display featured two couples, Mr and Mrs Ready and Mr and Mrs Unready. The former had bought a shopping bag from the store and so, according to the display, 'their shopping bags are conscience free'. The second couple by contrast had not been so wise as to buy a bag and so had to carry their purchases home wrapped in paper, a commodity in short supply during the war.

The store also supported the war effort by opening a National Savings Department for the sale of savings stamps and certificates.

Following the war the 1950s proved to be a decade of increased prosperity for the firm. TJ Hughes also continued to play its part in aiding the welfare of the nation: in 1955 the store set aside a space for a Welfare Foods Distribution Centre which stocked dried milk, cod

Right: TJ Hughes' distribution centre for national dried milk in 1955. Below: TJ Hughes' main window display during the second world war, showing how little stock there was to sell.

liver oil and orange juice. On a lighter note it was during the mid-1950s that Pinky and Perky the famous puppets and their Pop Parade first made a special appearance at

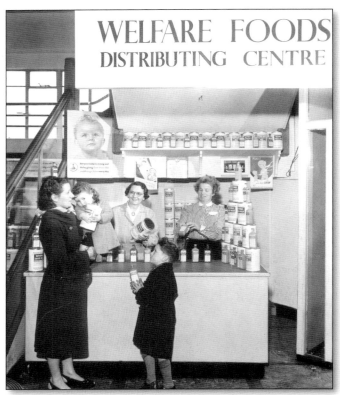

the store. The porky television personalities were at the store at Christmastime to help Father Christmas in providing entertainment for Liverpool's children. The show has been followed every Christmas since with ever more impressive decorations, displays and grottoes, including the unforgettable 'Dancing Waters' display of 1961.

The Welsh connection with the store was enthusiastically maintained down the decades. The staff wore daffodils on St David's Day right up until the 1960s. Every Thursday was designated Welsh Day, with coaches arriving from North Wales. Up until the 1970s, in order to avoid confusion with similar Welsh surnames only one member of staff with each name was allowed, and if a second person with the same name was started they were given another surname starting with the same letter!

The 1970s and 1980s were prosperous years. Yet that prosperity would be eclipsed by the achievements of the 1990s.

In the 1990s TJ Hughes started to open new outlets. The business grew to such an extent that it was able to become a publicly quoted company on the Stock Exchange as TJ Hughes plc.

Today TJ Hughes is going from strength to strength. With more and more stores opening across the country, TJ Hughes now has outlets from Dumfries to Eastbourne and occupies an enormous 2 million square feet. TJ Hughes has even become a shopping destination by having three out-of-town outlets in shopping villages across the UK. The stores themselves are also getting bigger and better with re-worked layouts and new store designs.

Now, almost 100 years after the foundation of the first small TJ Hughes shop the group now has 50 stores (with 20 of these opening just over the past decade). The company is one of Liverpool's great business success stories and, despite its size, continues to function as much an integral part of the city as it was in the early 20th Century when Thomas Hughes opened his modest draper's shop.

Although Thomas would, no doubt, be astounded at the extent of the company's growth, he would still recognise the store he created with its philosophy of exceptional value for money teamed with tight operating standards. The company's present Chief Executive, Robin Dickie, has kept TJ Hughes at the forefront of consumer's minds by maintaining the popular formula of offering brand names at discounted prices.

Employees and stores across the country are now looking forward to the TJ Hughes centenary in 2012 and, with new stores still opening across the country, another successful 100 years of trading!

Above: The store pictured in 1961, showing one of the famous Christmas grottos, 'Dancing Waters'.

GETRAG FORD Transmissions - All hail to Halewood!

The names 'Ford' and 'Halewood' will be inextricably linked for generations yet to come. In recent years however the Halewood Transmission Plant has been operated under the rather less familiar name of GETRAG FORD Transmissions – a joint business venture which is taking the celebrated plant forward into the 21st century.

For the younger generation the Halewood Transmission Plant had been part of the Liverpool scene forever: but when the Quarrymen first began to play Halewood was still an area of wild roses and strawberry fields.

Right: The building of Ford Halewood Transmission Plant in 1963. Below: An aerial view of Halewood Transmission Plant site, part of Ford's industrial estate which covers 346 acres to the south of Liverpool.

Nineteen sixty-four was a year to remember. Not only was it the 'year of the Beatles' but it was also the year of the Tokyo Olympic Games, the year Khrushchev was toppled as leader of the Soviet Union and China joined the 'atomic club' by exploding its first A-bomb.

For Britain the death of Sir Winston Churchill would shortly mark the end of an era, but for Liverpool a new era was just opening: the arrival of the Ford Motor Company at Halewood.

Two red roses picked on Midsummer's day were once the annual rent for the land on which the Halewood factory now stands. The blooms were handed over by the Ireland family to the area's wealthiest and most powerful landlord, Lord Derby. Lord Derby may well have chosen the peppercorn rent of flowers instead of money because he was tired of the endless bickering over land entitlement along the banks of the River Mersey to the south of Liverpool, with first one group and then another waving the 11th century equivalent of cheque books under his aristocratic nose. Or maybe he was just a keen rose lover who couldn't bother himself to cut the blooms for table decorations during a difficult early growing season.

Though some things about Halewood will remain a mystery forever, what is well known is that the annals of Halewood stretch back to well before the Norman Conquest of 1066. The area was part of the Great Lancashire Forest of the Saxon King Edward the

Confessor, and was rigorously preserved for Royal hunting. Through the years parts of Halewood - particularly the southern section which would be occupied by Ford – were the subject of bitter wrangles between the local farming gentry. But despite such disputes the area remained essentially a peaceful rural backwater until the 1960s when it emerged from its obscurity and was thrust into the front line of the car industry, and a new Battle of Britain – the battle for the automotive export market.

Ford planned to locate its very large expansion programme envisaged in the 1960s in Dagenham. The expansion would have dovetailed nicely into the excellent production facilities that already existed there. There was also a trained labour force used to the Ford pattern and methods of working, and a concentration which would have minimised costs and overheads. The Government however was insistent that expansion should be channelled into the distressed areas of Britain. When Ford announced its plans for Merseyside there were 27,000 unemployed in the

Above: Ray Knott operating a Talyrond measuring machine.

area and a substantial decline in many traditional labour-intensive industrial and commercial businesses.

The choice of Merseyside – Halewood – for an £8.5 million investment was made in September 1962 after detailed surveys had been carried out in a number of locations offered to Ford by the Board of Trade: Scotland, the North East, and South Wales (where Ford would in fact build a factory to produce rear axles for its passenger and commercial ranges).

Halewood was chosen for several reasons:

First the 346-acre site was ample not only for the proposed first phase of expansion but also allowed plenty of room for future developments. The site was also well supplied with gas, electricity, fuel oil and water. The estate was well served by a good network of communications: on the North side was the Liverpool to London railway line providing Ford, through special sidings, with rolling stock with a high speed 'conveyor line' between Halewood and Dagenham. Ford was the first to use the 'Blue trains', forerunners of the linertrains. Trains would plie between Halewood ad Dagenham every day bringing engines, rear axles and forgings and castings, and carrying away gearboxes, stampings and trim.

Halewood became one of the key distribution centres in Ford's national vehicle distribution system. Thirty-five trains would leave Halewood and Garston every week on 'cartics' and car flats for distribution points throughout the country. On the South side were good roads. The Speke Boulevard, built as a joint venture between Liverpool Corporation, Lancashire County Council and Ford, was

built to expressway standards. The plant would also be close to the M62, in turn linking to the M6 and M1.

The good roads provided an excellent and rapid route for suppliers, whilst also enabling employees to clear the plant in less than ten minutes at shift start up and finishing time. Good docking facilities at Garston and Liverpool, and by trans-Pennine rail to the north-east coast, were also a significant advantage. Liverpool Airport, less than a mile way, provided an ideal pick-up point for air-freighted supplies and a touchdown for executive travellers.

Against these advantages however had to be set some disadvantages.

The sheer distance from Dagenham created extra transport costs, whilst also facing the company with recruiting in an area which had no previous experience of the motor industry or of flow-production techniques.

To surmount the skills gap Ford established the largest and most comprehensive training programme ever undertaken by British industry - £2 million was spent on training before a single production car was built. In the initial stages Ford established a mock production line in an aircraft hanger at Liverpool Airport, where the first recruits were trained whilst the plant itself was being constructed. The first 30 Merseyside employees were recruited on 1st January 1962. As the plant progressed and machinery moved in training was established there. Altogether 8,000 workers were given operator training.

Left: *Margaret Thatcher, then leader of the Opposition was a VIP visitor to the plant in 1978.* **Above** *Presentation of Foremanship Certificates, April 1979.*

Part of the training was an induction programme in which each operator was introduced to the company and its managers, and given a comprehensive run down on Halewood's part in the Ford Motor Company's operations.

There was also a management development programme in which the new management team at Halewood –one of the youngest in the country – was sent on training courses tailored to suit individual's own particular needs. Another important part of the training programme was the trainee foreman scheme in which potential supervisors were given six months training on such subjects as work-study, industrial relations and communications.

To establish the training programme 300 key personnel from Dagenham (and later from Doncaster) were brought up to Halewood to train new recruits and establish a corps of experienced supervisors. The same pattern was repeated when the transmission plant was built at Heywood, only this time a special training centre was established at Kirkby.

The original factory was completed in 1964, constructed for the production and assembly of light, medium and heavy car transmissions.

The chosen site was adjacent to Ford's new Stamping and Assembly Plants (then under construction, and which would complete the first car made on Merseyside on 8th March1963).

*Above: Tommy Smith (the then plant manager) and Derek Smith present Henry Ford II with a memento of Merseyside on his visit to Halewood Transmission Plant. **Below**: Civil dignitaries from Liverpool, Knowsley and Halewood were guests when the production milestones of 10,000,000 gearboxes was reached.*

It was decreed that the Halewood Transmission Plant would be the most modern and technically advanced factory of its kind in the world, achieving maximum efficiency in the manufacturing process and making gearboxes for Ford's entire range of vehicles. No craftsman could hope to match the precision of the 2,000 production machines, far less the array of complex and costly equipment specifically installed to ensure consistently high standards of quality.

Construction took just 16 months from start to finish. It was one of the fastest plant building operations of its size ever to take place in Britain, as well as being one of the first in which the 'critical path' method of planning – hailed at the time as a revolutionary step – would be employed.

A special operations room, or 'command module' was set up on site to administer details of the construction, with a computer calculating the most effective and direct ways of building. Deadlines for completion of the various phases of construction together with manpower requirements and schedules for the supply of materials were also calculated. Alternative courses of action were planned for in case of any hold-up in the critical path due to bad weather or other unforeseeable factors.

Though many machines were new, hundreds more were transferred from Dagenham. As one Dagenham machine was shut down on a Friday night it was dismantled, shipped to Halewood and reassembled ready for use on the following Monday.

It was envisaged that the total plant personnel would be 3,000, with a daily output of more than one gearbox for every man and woman on the payroll.

A seven-bay extension was added to the east side of the building in 1966 to accommodate the production of chassis and steering components, increasing the total area of the plant to over a million square feet. A further two-bay expansion of 75,000 square feet was built in 1978 and 1979 on the plant's west side for the launch of the new front-wheel drive Escort transaxle in 1980 bringing the total area to 1.2 million square feet.

In the early 1970s the plant was making over 3,000 transmissions every day. Liverpool celebrated in 1978 when the three millionth Ford vehicle, an Escort, rolled off its Halewood production line.

In the dark days of the mid-1980s however production schedules at the plant were down to just 1,700 transmis-

sions a day. Yet despite apparent problems the plant was a place which most local people felt a great affinity and affection: On the plant's 25th birthday, its Silver Jubilee, in 1989 a head count revealed no fewer than 425 employees had each been with the firm since the day it had opened.

By the turn of the millennium Halewood had become a joint Ford-Jaguar site comprising a vehicle Assembly Plant and a Manual Transmissions Operations Plant. Historically the Body and Assembly Plant had been the mainstay for a variety of Ford models including Capri, Corsair and the Escort models. Investment was being planned to re-equip for prestigious Jaguar production with the whole site intended to employ 4,000 people, 3,000 aligned to the Jaguar Plant. By then the Manual Transmission Operations Plant was employing around 1,000 people. The workforce being organised through IMTs (Integrated Manufacturing Teams) made up of skilled and semi-skilled people embracing responsibility for production, part quality, facility maintenance and parts scheduling.

Ford had long recognised the quality of its workers, describing its 'prime asset' as 'the depth of automotive technical skill inherent within the local workforce...one of the most highly skilled and technically competent work forces in Europe'. Today the transmissions plant at Halewood employs around 800 staff. Since 1st February 2001 the plant has been operated by GETRAG FORD Transmissions

GETRAG FORD Transmissions was founded as a joint venture between the transmission specialist GETRAG, whose headquarters are in Untergruppen- bach (Baden-Württemberg), and the Ford Motor Company. The purpose

Left: *Celebrations as the 15 millionth transaxle is produced.*
Above: *Plant manager Bob Taylor receives the award for 2005 Best Engineering Plant.* **Right:** *HRH Prince Andrew visits the plant in 2005 to celebrate the many awards and achievements received by the company.*

of the joint venture is to combine the strengths of both partners in the field of manual and automated manual transmissions. In order to give the joint venture the best possible chances of business success, the parent companies contributed skilled personnel, a state-of-the-art product development centre, production plants and the necessary know-how and capital.

Since its foundation, the company has won several new customers, including Mazda, MG Rover and Volvo. The partners have combined their strengths and resources in order to ensure that this positive development is maintained.

As a systems supplier, the company's services include not only developing and producing transmissions, but also developing and delivering components and shifter controls, integrating transmission systems into vehicles and providing the engineering services.

With transmission technology and production, GETRAG FORD Transmissions continues to trust in its tried-and-tested manual and automated manual transmissions, which are constantly being adapted to current market requirements. Its development work also focuses on the driveline technologies of the future, including twin clutch and stepless transmissions, electric and hybrid drives and their control systems, which deliver unadulterated driving pleasure in an attractive all-in-one package.

Constant investment in forward-looking development concepts and state-of-the-art production technology forms the basis for the implementation of the company's vision. With dedication and determination its people at Halewood play an active role in shaping products and business processes, so contributing in a sustainable way to the firm's success. GETRAG FORD Transmissions also encourages employees to develop a new outlook within its Blue Sky initiative, the aim of which is to ensure an optimal position for the company with regard to the transmission and powertrain technologies of the future.

The Venmore Partnership - Helping homebuyers

The career span of one of the Venmore Partnership's former Senior Partners illustrates just how much the Liverpool-based property firm has grown in recent years.

Miles Pickering retired at the end of 2005 having seen the business develop significantly during his 33 years' service.

When he first joined what was formerly W & J Venmore it only had three offices, but today the Venmore Partnership can boast more than 20 estate agency branches across the region.

The Partnership is the largest independent firm of chartered surveyors, estate agents, valuers, auctioneers, and property managers in the North West. As well as being the fifth largest auctioneers in the UK and the biggest outside London, it is also the 25th largest estate agents in the country.

Top: James Venmore, founder partner of W&J Venmore.
Right: Miles Pickering gaining entry to Kemlyn Road - the last house to be vacated prior to their client, Liverpool Football Club, building the Centenary Stand on the site.

In 2005 they sold £300m worth of properties.

Venmore, however, is a name known for more than just its business activities.

Venmore's staff work hard organising and supporting charity events and have raised an impressive £55,500 for local and national charities in just over 12 months.

But to find the roots of the Venmore Partnership you have to go back more than a century and a half.

The original firm of Thomas & Jones was founded in the 1850s and the founding partners were estate agents in the original sense of the words.

They managed rows of terraced houses collecting the rent, organising repairs, dealing with re-letting and acting on behalf of the owners.

Both founders were Welsh and they worked for the many Welsh builders who were then active in Liverpool.

Mr Thomas left within four years but Mr Jones continued to expand the business. During the inter-war years he briefly took his son into the firm, but that association did not last.

In the 1930s the business was acquired by a Mr Russell who took a Mr Lloyd-Jones into partnership after the Second World War.

They continued until the mid-1950s when Mr Russell retired and Mr Lloyd Jones died suddenly soon afterwards.

For some time the business was run by Peter Jones, who started as an assistant in 1959, and office manager George Morgan on behalf of Lloyd-Jones' widow, and eventually this pair bought the firm.

Mike Earl joined in 1960 at a time when the firm was

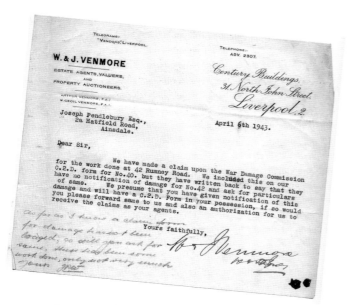

George Morgan retired in 1973, four years after Mike Earl had become a partner. In 1976 Thomas & Jones acquired the firm of Patterson & Thomas, from whom David Jones was to join the Partnership.

Patterson & Thomas was founded in 1849 and for much of its existence had occupied a Grade One listed building in Cook Street. Thomas & Jones were next door, and so a bridge was built between the two buildings. The merger meant that Thomas & Jones now included commercial property work as part of the practice and David Jones and David Inman dealt with this part of the business.

Meanwhile the survey business had expanded and Derek Coates joined as a partner in the mid 1970s.

The firm's Drawing Office and Building Surveying side had grown from a tiny start following the earlier purchase of Herbert Davis, but that side of the business would split away from Thomas & Jones in the 1980s.

It was also in this decade that discussions with the firm of W&J Venmore led to the amalgamation of the two firms into Venmore, Thomas & Jones.
W&J Venmore had taken its name from twin brothers William and James Venmore sons of the High Sheriff of Anglesey. In the late 19th Century they had established an estate agents business in Liverpool's Scotland Road. James would actually follow in his father's footsteps to become High Sheriff of Anglesey.

James Venmore's sons, Arthur and Cecil, would carry on the family business after the deaths of their father and uncle who, curiously, died within eight hours of each other in December 1920.

expanding, mainly by providing valuation and survey services to Building Societies.

The Partnership acquired several small property management businesses in the 1960s including that of Herbert Davies in Birkenhead which took the firm into a new area of business - design work.

Peter Jones was also involved with the formation of the Liver Housing Association in 1966 when a group of professionals came together to help provide quality rented housing. He was joined by, among others, Lawrence Jones of Thomas R Jones and Sons solicitors, Mr R Black of Page, Burne and Black accountants and local MP Richard Crawshaw.

By the end of its first 25 years the Association would be receiving annual income in rents of almost £6 million from hundreds of new homes.

*Top right: A letter dated April 1943 from W. & J. Venmore acting as agents for a claim upon the War Damage Commission. **Left and below:** War damaged houses in Carrisbrook Road (left) and Berwyn Road.*

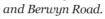

They were joined in 1936 by C Roger Morton. Arthur and Cecil died in 1961 and 1974 respectively and Roger, who had won a VC during the war, ran the partnership with the third generation of the Venmore family, Neville Venmore, until Neville's death in 1972.

Miles Pickering then joined the firm which was going from strength to strength helped by Roger's deep local knowledge.

It was following Roger's retirement that, due to the size of the firm, Miles Pickering had to seek assistance, which resulted in the amalgamation with Thomas & Jones.

In Southport, the firm of Ball & Percival had been established in 1900 by Walter Knight Ball and a Mr Percival but their partnership split up early on leaving just Walter.

An advert in a local newspaper in 1900 refers to him having previously had 11 years' experience with a firm called Hindle & Son. The new business was established as a firm of auctioneers, valuers, estate and insurance agents, mortgage brokers and accountants with offices at St George's Place.

In 1905 the business relocated to the premises it still occupies in Lord Street.

Raymond Knight Ball, one of Walter Ball's sons, took over the firm on his father's retirement in the 1930s, and in the 1940s the first non-family members became partners. Raymond Ball retired in 1964, a year after Bruce Jones joined the firm.

It continued to prosper as an independent partnership and in 1986 it became a limited company and was taken over by Hambro Countrywide Plc, the largest estate agency chain in the country.

Hambro's initial philosophy was to retain established trading names, and the business continued to trade as Ball & Percival. In 1988 however, there was a name change, followed by a subsequent decline for the business which was, by then, operating from five more offices at Tarleton, Ainsdale, Formby, Ormskirk and Burscough - plus a short-lived seventh at Crosby.

Bruce Jones resigned his directorship on the change of name at the end of 1988 and with a business colleague he established a property consultancy. He bought back the professional side of the former Ball & Percival business in 1990, trading from 21 Hoghton Street in Southport.

Top left: Details for the auction of numbers 1 to 65 Anglesey Street, Bootle in 1923. Top right: Lots for auction in the 1920s. Below left: The firm's Lord Street, Southport, office. Below: An advertisement for Ball and Percival, 1900.

In 1991 he was concerned to see his former business in decline, and though still occupying its four-storey building it was only utilising the ground floor. A buy-back of what was left of the business was agreed later that year.

At the same time Ball & Percival, now led by Bruce Jones, merged with the even longer established practice of Venmore, Thomas & Jones in Liverpool.

Simon Wall joined the original Ball & Percival in November 1988 and became a Partner in 1999 following Peter Jones' retirement in the July. Philip Cassidy joined the Partnership and took over Peter's role as auctioneer and was able to enhance the already successful auction department. The six-weekly auctions would see sales of more than 1,000 properties annually.

A number of the Partners are also Directors of Colette Gunter Ltd, Formby's most experienced estate agents, and of Venmore Thomas and Jones (Prescot) Ltd with offices in and around the St Helens and Warrington areas.

Simon Wall became managing partner following the retirement of Bruce Jones and has been overseeing the development and expansion of the business during the last few years.

2003 saw Venmores moving to newly refurbished headquarters in the former Radio City premises in Stanley Street, Liverpool City centre.

The Venmore Partnership's status as the largest independent firm of estate agents in the North West continues to grow having formed a partnership with Brian Phillips of Phillips & Sons.

Phillips & Sons' two established estate agency branches in Bootle and Netherton have joined Venmore's 21 other branches in Merseyside, Lancashire and Cheshire.

Phillips & Sons began as Bootle Estate Office, also on Stanley Road, founded in 1925 by Brian's grandfather and business partner Mr T. Woosnam Roberts.

Following further restructuring of the practice during 2005, which would eventually see the firm transfer in to a Limited Liability Partnership (LLP), it also saw the promotion of a number of the firm's associates to Partner level with Phil Furlong taking on responsibility for all Liverpool estate agencies, and Karen Potter, taking on the Ball & Percival offices in and around Southport. David Blackman also became a Partner working with Simon Wall overseeing the property management department. Stephanie Macnab and Nigel Lowsby were also promoted to Associates.

But as faces change progress remains a constant feature. In 2006 a new Venmore Thomas & Jones office opened in the historical setting of Liverpool's Woolton Village. Meanwhile the Venmore Partnership, has grown even larger by joining forces with Liverpool's leading commercial property agency, and professional services firm Dears Brack.

Dears Brack has more than 20 years of experience in the commercial property market and are also experts in project management.

Venmore's Managing Partner Simon Wall said: 'We have over 155 years of experience in the residential property market and a very successful auction house. Dears Brack are renowned as commercial property specialists and property consultants. Together we believe we are unbeatable in the breadth of our offer and we look forward to a prosperous future together'.

"With the expanded range of services available, our list of Partners has also increased. With the merger we welcomed Peter Brack, David Strettle, Mark Hardie, Kevin Cockburn and Stephen Sands as Partners."

Dears Brack residential property clients moved over to Venmore's thriving City estate agency branch on Stanley Street while the commercial arm of the business continues at Dears Brack's North John Street office.

What a long and complex history... It's been a very busy six or seven years, but Venmore's continues to look to the future, with expansion plans well under way for at least a further three offices before the end of 2006.

Above: The Venmore Partnership group photograph, 2006.
Inset: The firm's Stanley Street premises.

Arena Housing - Homes for life

Over the last 40 years most of the City's older housing has either disappeared or been renovated, much of that work has been down to housing associations. The Arena Housing Group based in Liverpool currently manages over 13,000 houses and flats in the North West predominately in Liverpool, Chester, Knowsley, Sefton, St Helens, Warrington, Wigan and Wirral. The Group also operates specialist divisions in supported care which provides services to supported housing residents including Foyers and Homesless hostels and ExtraCare which provides homes and services for older residents. The Group also operates 2 retirement villages in Warrington and St Helens with a third being built in Sheffield.

Although the Arena name has only been existence since 2001 following the merger of Grosvenor and Liver Housing Associations, Liver's roots go back to the swinging sixties and Grosvenor's to the early 1970s.

Liver Housing Association was formed in 1966 when a group of professionals came together to provide quality rented housing at a time of shortage. Following the formation the Association played an important role

working in partnership with Liverpool City Council and the Housing Corporation providing affordable homes mainly in the Liverpool area. Throughout its existence Liver was successful in building and improving homes through the coupling of its social aims and the vision of its Board of unpaid volunteers. One of the Association's first developments at "Sunnyside" is situated off Devonshire Road and forms a small cul-de-sac on the edge of Princes Park. There have been houses in

Top: May Place formerly St Vincent's Hospice in 1923.
Above: May Place, Liver's sheltered scheme on Broadgreen Road.

"Sunnyside" since the later part of the 19th Century when Liverpool was enjoying the wealth created by its links with the colonies and North America. The Buildings in "Sunnyside" therefore form an important part of Liverpool's architectural heritage.

During the early 1980s the Association recognised that its older residents whom it had housed in the sixties and seventies would require sheltered accommodation. With this in mind the Association enlarged its role to create a subsidiary which provided accommodation with care and support for the elderly and by 1996 the Association had six well staffed homes.

In 1989 Liver acquired 700 properties in the Brookvale estate in Runcorn and over the following three years undertook a major programme of repairs including initiating a wide ranging environmental improvement programme. The Association during this period also bought properties in Runcorn Old Town, Widnes and Brookvale.

Grosvenor's history as already stated goes back to the early 1970s building its first schemes in St Helens and moving to other areas such as Wigan and Manchester in the 1970s. Grosvenor's history largely follows a similar path to Liver In 1992 they took on the management of over 800 properties from the Commission for New Towns in Warrington following a ballot of residents of which 74 percent voted in favour of the transfer.

Grosvenor made great inroads in the development of housing for the elderly and at its 20th anniversary in 1996 had built over 18 sheltered schemes which amounted to 567 homes, the first one being built in Thatto Heath in 1981.

Young people were also part of the housing equation, and the Association in the 1980s embarked on a comprehensive programme of providing accommodation for young

single people at a time when it was not necessarily the most popular client group; once again at its 20th anniversary in 1996 they had six schemes exclusively for young people totalling 400 units.

It was during the late 1990s that Grosvenor and Liver started to look at how they could, working together develop Arena Housing Association to provide more affordable homes for those people who required them but also make a real contribution to the communities which they served.

Whilst both Associations share a long history it is in property rehabilitation that the Association made its greatest impact. There is a history of street rehabilita-

Below: An aerial view of the plaza in front of the Anglican Cathedral during the development of Liver's Cathedral Mews and Alfred Mews (circa 1990).

tion throughout Merseyside a need rooted in the problems associated with private housing which is mainly of the pre 1919 vintage. In the late 1970s the Housing Corporation had invested substantial amounts of money in rehabilitating funding which was linked to housing action area programmes. Local Authorities would offer landlords improvement grants, compulsory purchasing those properties which had not been improved within the statutory time limit. Such purchases were then vested in housing associations for them to make improvements.

Once such area in which Arena has a large number of properties requiring substantial investment is

Top: Tenement buildings in Old Swan during clearance in the mid 1990s. **Above: both pictures:** *Liver property on Canning Street both before and after renovation.*

Anfield/Breckfield. The long term decline in the housing market in the area has resulted in wide-scale abandonment and the turnover of properties has led to the area having a vacant property rate 50 percent above the city wide average. However, despite all its problems the Anfield/Breckfield area still presents attractive opportunities for redevelopment. Arena is working with the two premiership clubs Everton and Liverpool and the community to develop real opportunities for breathing new life into the Anfield/Breckfield area.

Indeed the idea of bringing new life into the area is the idea for an initiative which Arena is now leading on in the area. LIFE, short for Lead, Influence, Follow and Exit is being implemented by all Associations in the current four Housing Market Renewal Areas of Liverpool which have similar problems to Anfield/Breckfield. This LIFE initiative will allow Arena, working with residents and its partners, to focus skills and resources to ensure that the

Anfield/Breckfield area continues to thrive and move on from its current problems.

In Sefton the Association worked with Bootle Maritime City Challenge to produce new homes by Strand Road and began the regeneration of the Bootle Village. In Rock Ferry, parts of that property were converted into accommodation to be used by young single mothers and women at risk. Whilst for people with disabilities the Association installed showers and stair lifts in their properties.

In Liverpool's Old Swan district the tenements at St Oswald House, St Oswald Gardens and Hurst Gardens were in a state of disrepair. The buildings had been erected by the City Council immediately after the second world war. A total of approximately 150 homes have been built in the Old Swan as part of Project Orchid. One particular element was the redevelopment of St Vincent's Hospice on Broad Green Road were the Association developed the sheltered housing scheme May Place, preserving the façade of this grade 2 listed building.

As well as being involved in the regeneration of Anfield/Breckfield inevitably the Association has also been prominent in the regeneration of other parts of the city such as the Canning area which is the largest area of Georgian housing in the North West of England. In this area the Association was given the task of acquiring and improving a number of listed buildings and the Association has been able to acquire a number of properties for conversion into flats at affordable rents. Properties in Canning Street for example were acquired from Liverpool City Council in a dilapidated condition and have undergone a complete refurbishment, the cost being met jointly the housing association, Housing Corporation and English Heritage.
Bringing the story of the Arena Group up to present day, in 2004 Liverpool City Council residents of Sefton Park confirmed their wish to transfer to the Arena Housing Group and in total 350 tenants were transferred along with 67 leaseholders.

In 2005 St Helens Housing Association joined the Arena Group. Currently the Arena Group is developing four further Extra Care housing schemes in Liverpool, Sefton and Knowsley and it is hoped that a retirement village will become a reality in the Anfield/Breckfield area over the coming years.

Arena Housing Association whilst young in its origins has a long history behind it of developing homes for people in Liverpool and the greater Merseyside region. The first 30 years of each of these Associations lives has been a real challenge, the next 30 years hold even greater challenges for the Arena Housing Group but it is well placed to rise to these challenges and make a real difference to peoples lives now and in the future.

Top left: Mosslake, apartments built for shared ownership sale on the site of the former Catholic Apostolic Church on the corner of Canning Street and Catherine Street. Left: One of Arena's residents who took part in the annual gardening competition. Below: New properties in Lansdowne Place, Anfield.

Yorkshire Copper Tube - A pipe dream come true

Yorkshire Copper Tube's vast brick building on the East Lancashire Road, Kirkby bas been a local landmark for more than half a century.

The company, part of the KME group, manufactures copper plumbing tube for the UK market and for export around the world.

In recent years, there bas been a continuing programme of investment in the factory to keep it in the forefront of tube producing technology. Such have been the improvements in efficiency that the numbers employed today are but a fraction of the 2,000 once employed, yet the plant's output is greater than ever. These efficiency improvements have been very necessary to maintain Yorkshire Copper Tube's position in a highly competitive market.

The company's roots can be traced back to the Broughton Copper Company founded in Salford in 1864.

ICI Metals Ltd bought the Broughton Copper Co in 1934 and after the end of the second world war, began looking for a site for a new factory. The site ICI found was in Kirkby, Liverpool - a decision said to have been strongly influenced by local Labour MP Harold Wilson. It had been impossible to extend the Broughton Copper Works' original manufacturing unit in Manchester, since it was bounded by the River Irwell which on several occasions had burst its banks and flooded both the works and nearby streets. In 1948 Kirkby was selected because it offered several advantages which could not be matched by any other location in the region.

Firstly, the Government had designated a large part of Kirkby as an industrial estate and was actively encouraging industry to move there with the aid of grants.

Secondly, the new town of Kirkby was in the first stages of development and many of the people of Merseyside were moving out to its new homes and to new jobs in what was then still very much the countryside. The New Town in particular, and Merseyside in general, offered a vast reservoir of labour which it was felt would be readily attracted to the good conditions and advantages being offered by the new factory, particularly as the area was troubled by a level of unemployment significantly higher than the national average.

Top: *Early company vehicles.*
Left: *The Kirkby Works in the 1950s..*

the motorway network, greatly facilitating transport to and from the site.

Work began on the new plant in 1948. The main buildings were completed and the first tubes produced within two years. The factory was not finally completed, however, until 1955 and was then able to manufacture all the copper and alloy tubes for ICI's Metals Division. The factory was the largest copper tube producing unit in Europe, rivalled only by even newer non-ferrous companies in the USA. Indeed, at a third of a mile long, the factory is thought to be the longest brick building in Europe.

Some personnel were transferred from Broughton to work in the new factory: they received 'key worker' certificates which gave them priority access to the new houses being built in Kirkby.

Thirdly, from a communication point of view, the site was unique. Liverpool docks offered a convenient means of importing copper and were also a gateway to world markets for the finished products. The East Lancashire Road has since increased in importance as a route and the busy road now gives direct access to

The creation of a new factory in Kirkby presented a once in a lifetime opportunity for the planners to start from scratch. During the preceding 20 years technical advances in tube manufacture had been rendering the traditional short drawbenches obsolete. It was,

Top: *An aerial view of the Kirkby Works , 1950s.*
Above : *'C Bay' extension in 1964.*

therefore, decided that the most satisfactory production method would be to manufacture all mass production items in a single length wherever practicable in order to avoid the unnecessary cutting which was associated with 'bench lengths'. Bull-blocks were installed in order to maximise the lengths over which tube could be drawn and thus overcome problems of handling long lengths of tube.

Drawbenches were still used for many stages of production but the plant was laid out in a straight 'flow line', a then unique feature in the British tube making industry, which had previously manufactured tubes in batches, with each batch moving in a different direction between each stage of production.

By the mid-1950s the ICI Metals Division and its competitor, the Yorkshire Copper Works in Leeds, between them supplied almost 90 per cent of the UK's requirements for copper and copper alloy tubing and it was rapidly becoming clear that the market could not support two similar large enterprises.

The answer to both companies' problems was a merger which married the Leeds company's special expertise

Right: The Kirkby Works, pictured in the 1960s.
Below: A view down the factory in the 1960s: coiled tube being transferred by a rigid mast crane to storage arms.

in both tube and fittings with ICI Metals' large-scale production capacity. In 1958 Yorkshire Imperial Metals was formed, jointly owned by the ICI Metals division and the Leeds-based Yorkshire Copper Works. The Kirkby works became part of this new company.

In 1965, ICI Metals Division, by now known as IMI, became 100 percent owners of Yorkshire imperial Metals and, in 1977, IMI was floated off from ICI. In 1983 Yorkshire Copper Tube was set up as a separate company within IMI, based at the Kirkby site. From this date the sales and marketing function, previously based at Leeds, was transferred to Kirkby and the company increasingly specialised in mass-production plumbing tube.

The tube-forming process originally begins with a piercing operation on a hot copper 'billet', extruding it into a 'shell' which can then be drawn out into a tube. The first press, of 2,500 tonnes, was installed in the mid-1950s, followed by a second press of 3,500 tonnes in 1964. The current press of 5,000 tonnes was installed in 1981.

The original drawing processes, as already noted, involved drawbenches and bull-blocks. Following an extensive £30 million investment programme in the late 1980s and early 1990s, the factory was re-equipped with state-of-the-art Schumag CDM drawing machines and spinner blocks, which are used to draw out the pierced and extruded billets to their final dimensions. At the same time, sophisticated new automatic tube handling equipment was installed.

In the early years, the Kirkby plant included a casting shop which produced copper billets from raw copper. During the mid-1960s, the introduction of semi-continuous casting improved billet quality and yield by eliminating impurities from slag during the casting process. However, in 1982 the casting shop was closed when it was realised that the plant at Kirkby had become outdated and that it would be cheaper to buy in copper billets.

One of the most significant technical developments in the 1960s was the introduction of 'bright annealing', which softens the tube to allow manipulation while preserving a bright, clean, shiny finish. This new process was a more cost effective way of annealing the tubes than the method formerly used and it was introduced in order to improve competitiveness against foreign manufacturers. The bright annealing process led to the introduction of new methods of tube cleaning to remove traces of carbon which can cause corrosion when exposed to cold water.

In December 2002 Yorkshire Copper Tube entered a new phase of its life when ownership transferred from IMI to KME, the largest producer of copper and copper alloy materials in Europe.

Today Yorkshire Copper Tube offers its customers a wide range of plain, plastic-coated and special finish copper tube for diverse applications including gas, heating water and sanitation systems. The key to the company's longevity is quality - quality so outstanding that the company confidently offers customers a remarkable 25-year guarantee on its products.

Above: *The Spinner Block.*
Below: *An aerial view of the factory, 2006.*

Merchant Taylors' Schools - Four centuries of learning

'Education, education, education' is a familiar modern mantra, but the desire to get a good education is an ancient and honourable one. Education has always been the key to a successful life, and because of that fact those who have found success in life almost invariably look back to 'the happiest days of their lives' and give due credit to the academic institutions which helped forge their characters.

Generations of Merseyside folk have been fortunate in being able to obtain an excellent education locally since the reign of James I.

Merchant Taylors' Schools, Crosby, was founded as a grammar school for boys by John Harrison in 1620, the year in which the Pilgrim Fathers first settled in New England.

Today the schools are led by a new Chair of Governors, Leo Colligan, appointed in 2005. A new headmaster, David Cook, joined the school in September 2005 followed in April 2006 by the appointment of a new headmistress of the girls' school, Louise Robinson.

In the years between its founding and today the original school has become four schools: a combined co-educational prep school and junior girls' school known as Stanfield, a boys' junior school, and two senior schools situated on separate sites - one each for boys and girls.

Top: The old school which was built in 1620 to house 60 boys is still in use today as part of the girls' school library and six form study area. *Below:* The whole school pictured in 1871 outside the old school house.

Single sex education is at the core of the schools, but boys and girls share some A level subjects in sixth form.

Founder John Harrison was a member of the Merchant Taylors' Company in London where he owned considerable amounts of land, as well as in Yorkshire, Berkshire and Essex.

The 'Guild and Fraternity of St. John the Baptist, time out of mind called tailors and linen armourers of London' had been in existence since at least in 1300 when it was recorded that 'they chose Henry de Ryall to be their pilgrim'. Letters Patent of Edward III issued in 1327 record Royal acceptance of the Guild in its first Charter.

The commonly used phrase 'all at sixes and sevens' meaning, 'all confused', or 'in disagreement', stems from the days when the Merchant Taylors' Company and the Merchant Skinners' Company were unable to agree amongst themselves as to which of the two ancient companies was the more senior – in 1484 Richard III was seeking to put his Guilds into ranking order; the Lord Mayor of London, one Billesden's, wise Soloman-like solution to the

disagreement was that one year the Taylors' were ranked sixth, with the Skinners seventh, and vice versa the following year. This is known as the principle of 'sixes and sevens'. Of course this hardly resolved the question, but it provided a fitting solution to the disagreement!

Between 1512 and 1620 there had already been five schools and colleges established by Merchant Taylors the company in England and Ireland – now there was about to be a sixth.

John Harrison's father came from Great Crosby, and for several years before his death, John had it in mind to build and endow a free grammar school in his father's home village - for teaching, educating and instructing children and youth in the grammar and rules of learning forever.

Top: *A new classroom of 1912.*
Left: *An informal staff photograph of some members taken between 1904 and 1910. From bottom left, clockwise: Miss Mackenzie, Miss Mason, Miss Malpas, Miss Birchall, Mrs Burrows and Miss Mallaker.*

When he died, Harrison left enormous assets, part of which was bequeathed to the Merchant Taylors' Company to act as Trustees for his school in Crosby, a role they would retain until 1910.

The first Headmaster was the Revd John Kidde, followed (amongst others) by men still very much part of the School life who give their names to Houses or buildings, such as John Stevens, John Waring, Wilfred Troutbeck, Samuel Armour, Thomas York, and Mark Luft.

The original building still stands in Crosby, as part of Merchant Taylors' School for Girls (MTGS) - founded in 1888 - but is hidden from view by the newer buildings on Liverpool Road. Recently refurbished the 1620s building is the oldest school building still in use in Sefton.

In Canon Armour's time the School, sponsored for three centuries by one of the most important of the London City companies, had the chance to expand and develop. It grew into an important day school, to stand, with the benefit of its ancient foundation, on an equal footing with the best ancient public schools in the country .

In 1878, the Boys' School moved to an imposing new building, which has always been a famous landmark in Crosby, on the Liverpool to Southport A565 road. It is a fine example of Victorian architecture, with its imposing clock tower, which dominates the surrounding landscape.

The Girls' school opened in 1888 with 12 pupils and has grown ever since. At its opening the Girls' school boasted an all graduate female teaching staff, something which at the time was very rare as only four universities were granting degrees to women.

In 1988, to celebrate the centenary for the girls' the school played host to Prince Andrew and Sarah Duchess of York.

At this time the new centenary hall was built and new facilities developed for science, modern languages and home economics.

The school's profile was underlined in 2005 when one pupil, Gayathri Kumar, became the first BBC 'Hardspell' Champion.

Academically MTGS has been consistently placed amongst the top schools in the North-West – it has also achieved outstanding sporting achievements in areas such as hockey. Though MTGS has always had an academic tradition, its pupils are now able to sample numerous extra curricular activities. Music was mentioned in the last inspection for its excellence.

As for younger students, Stanfield is the Merchant Taylors' mixed prep school and also junior school for girls. It is located on its own site in between the Boys' and Girls' Senior schools sites. It has been in this current position since 1946, and has during recent years seen major redevelopment with a new building. Pupils are able to use the senior schools' facilities such as the swimming pool at the Boys' school.

Throughout the twentieth century, the School has moved with the times - making the successful transition from Public School to Direct Grant, and in due course, to Independent status. Most recently, the abolition of the Government Assisted Places Scheme has been faced by the introduction of some places funded by the Schools' Burseries.

Top: The Tennis Team, 1926. Pictured from left to right, back row: Peggy Grant, Ethel Hiller-Hughes, Doris Gerrard, front row: Joan Williams (Vice Captain) Hazel Thornton (Captain) and Lillian Kenworthy.
Left: A famous landmark in Crosby, the Victorian School opened in 1878 by the Countess of Derby.

Following the expansion of the Prep to two-form entry, in early 1998 Alan Hansen, former Liverpool football star (whose son started in the Preparatory department at MTS in 1988), opened the new classroom block and enlarged hall for the Prep - which was at the same time re-named as the Merchant Taylors' Junior School. An appeal was launched in the summer of 1998 to fund further building within both the boys' and girls' schools, and to provide endowed bursaries as replacements for the previous Assisted Places Scheme. The appeal raised no less than a million pounds to fund buildings and bursaries.

The Girls' and Boys' Schools' have faced up to the future of competitive education, and succeeded in consistently maintaining the best academic results in Merseyside (and indeed beyond, in the North-West). During previous inspections the Schools' have been commended with a glowing report as being outstanding in its many achievements, not just academically, but also in its many extra-curricular activities: music, drama, sport, Combined Cadet Force, and through the many societies which give pupils a chance to experience far more of life than just that inside the classroom.

As the Schools' motto 'Concordia parvae res crescunt' says - 'small things grow in harmony' - so the Schools' whole ethos is that its warm, and friendly atmosphere fosters the best which pupils have to offer, developing them to their full potential, and preparing them for the challenges of the modern world beyond. For some that personal preparation includes participation in such challenging extra-curricular

things as rowing and sailing. There are nearly 250 boys and girls involved in the Combined Cadet Force: in addition to weekly training, they have the opportunity of attending a variety of camps and courses, both in Great Britain and overseas. Mountaineering, camping, sailing, flying and shooting are just some of the activities in which they can get involved. Both boys and girls are encouraged to take part in the Duke of Edinburgh Award Scheme and many achieve success in Bronze, Silver and Gold awards.

The schools also play an active role in the local community, and carry out many fundraising activities for local charities such as Alder Hey, NSPCC.

*Top left: Year 1 girls from Merchant Taylors' Girls Junior School - Stanfield pose for a photograph for the 1953 prospectus brochure. **Top right:** Head Girls from Merchant Taylors' Girls' School (inset), 2006. **Below:** Studying at the Boys' School, 2006.*

Balfour Beatty - A powerful tale

Today Balfour Beatty Rail Projects is currently working on many high-profile rail projects both overseas and in the UK including Heathrow Terminal 5, the modernisation of the London Underground and the West Coast main line railway.

The company's electrification design office, based at Stephenson House in Kirkby, has its origins in two 19th century pioneering electrical cable companies. Callenders of Firth (formed in 1882) and British Insulated Wire Company of Prescot (formed in 1890), and one pioneering general electrical company, Balfour Beatty (formed in 1909).

The patent for paper-insulated cable was brought back from New York by James Atherton in 1889. Wrapping electric wires with paper rather than rubber was a safer, more effective and cheaper way of insulating copper wires. It would also rival the well-established Vulcanised

Bitumen type cable being made by Callenders of Firth. In 1890 James Atherton and his brother Jacob joined T P Hewitt, Managing Director of the Lancashire Watch Company, Colonel Pilkington of St Helens, and Sebastian de Ferranti the Liverpool-born electrical genius. They established a factory in Prescot.

The partners leased a large plot of land close to Prescot Station from King's College Cambridge. The building was completed in 1891. The London and North Western Railway Company provided a rail siding.

The **British Insulated Wire Company** supplied power to Knowsley Hall, the home of the Earl of Derby, one of the first houses in

Top: An early view of The British Insulated Wire Co's premises. Above: The Atherton brothers.

Callender's original company imported bitumen from Trinidad which it used in its cabling process. It also imported asphalt from Switzerland and it is claimed that the company was responsible for introducing asphalt for road making into England. The company was soon engaged in road-making, not only in England but also in Europe where it had contracts in Romania and in Russia. Whilst visiting St Petersburg in the early 1880s Tom Callender went to the opera where he was impressed to see the new Jablochkoff electric candles being used inside the building.

About this time, Tom Callender visited James Irvine & Company of Liverpool where he was handed a lump of elasticon which he was told was a waste product and was asked if he had any use for it. Experimenting with bitumen and elasticon William Callender produced a material which he called Vulcanised Bitumen.

During the 1880s Callenders supplied and installed cable in towns and cities all over England including the new Law Courts and Covent Garden Opera House in London, as well as distant places such as Sydney and Gibraltar. In the 1890s clients also included gold mines in South Africa as well as shipping orders to India and Hong Kong.

the country to have electric lights. The company also set up electric street-lights in Prescot.

The Prescot firm went on to become a world leader in railway electrification. Cables made in the factory went all over the world; the company also provided cables for the London Underground.

Locally the Liverpool and Prescot Light Railway cabled by the British Insulated Wire Company originally took its power from the works. The works power station also provided the public electricity for Prescot, Roby and Huyton until 1933. Raw copper generally came by road from Liverpool docks and until the mid-1950s the ancient red steam lorries of the Kirkdale Haulage Company were a familiar part of the Liverpool scene as they puffed their way to Prescot.

For the first half of the 20th century so many people worked at the factory that it had its own fire brigade, hospital, nurses, clubs and football team. The factory had its own road and a steam railway. When the factory's whistle blew at the end of each shift it was heard all over Prescot.

During the second world war the factory had its own Air Raid Wardens, and many local women worked at the factory doing heavy jobs while the men were away.

Top: *A view of one of the machine shops in 1899, where components for cable jointing and tramway overhead equipment were made. The company became a major supplier of cables, overhead trolley wire and fittings for electric tramways around the world.*
Above left: *Sir Thomas Callender.*
Below: *The factory fire brigade pictured in 1931.*

In 1888 came several major contracts in London and Liverpool, not least the Liverpool Electric Light Supply Company which was to be acquired by Liverpool Corporation in 1896. In 1889 cables for Buckingham Palace were laid into Queen Victoria's drawing room.

An interesting private installation completed by Callenders at the turn of the century was Bruce Ismay's residence in Cheshire. His company was the White Star Line and he travelled on all its ship's maiden voyages, not least that of the Titanic which he survived.

Another installation was at Pilkington Glass Works which led to Callenders being given the Liverpool power contract. Callenders opened an office in Liverpool at 36 Dale Street in 1889.

Tom Callender met Jacob Atherton of British Insulated Wire in 1900 at the first meeting of the Cable Makers' Association.

Between 1896 and 1901 Callenders supplied and laid cables for two of the earliest underground electrified railways for the Central London and the City & South London Railway. The company began its largest tramway contract with the electrification of London Metropolitan Tramways in 1902. By the end of the tramway era Callenders had carried out almost 50 contracts in the UK and overseas. In 1919 Callenders installed cables for Mersey Docks & Harbour Board and the GPO in Liverpool.

Callenders had some common interests with Balfour Beatty, particularly private electric power generation, whilst Callenders had investments in the Tramways Light & Power Company owned by Balfour Beatty. In 1969 this connection would lead to what was by then British Insulated Callenders Cables acquiring Power Securities (formed by George Balfour in 1922) of which Balfour Beatty was major part.

Meanwhile in 1924 Callenders began its first overseas railway electrification contract for the Bombay, Baroda and Central Indian Railway and also worked in Agra, the location of the Taj Mahal.

Callenders' construction interests spread to include power distribution networks, submarine cables, telephone cables, tramways, trolleybuses, railway signalling, cable bridges and masts and towers to carry cables across rivers and canals. Callenders supplied lighting and high-tension ignition cables for use in road vehicles and for traffic lights in the late 1920s.

During the 1930s the company benefited from the construction of the National Grid following the 1926 Electricity Act.

Above: George Balfour (left) and Andrew Beatty.
Below: Callender Cables working on London Metropolitan Tramways.

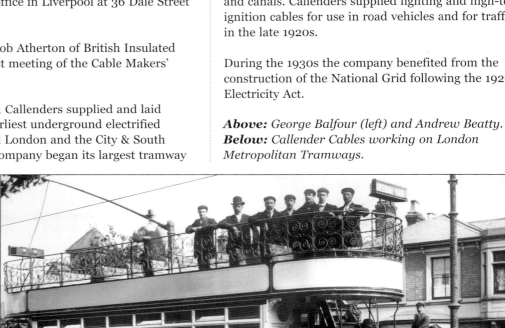

BICC began electrifying the UK West Coast main line railway in the early 1960s, completing it in 1966. The contract to electrify the Crewe to Glasgow route came in 1969.

In 1969 BICC bought the shares of Power Securities. This led to Balfour Beatty becoming part of BICC. In the 1970s BICC Construction was renamed Balfour Beatty Power Construction Ltd.

During the course of 1999, BICC was radically restructured through the disposal of its cable businesses and in May 2000 the Group changed its name to Balfour Beatty plc.

Callenders at Firth and WT Glover of Trafford Park (then part of the Callender Group) both played an important part in the manufacture of PLUTO (Pipe Line Under the Ocean) which played a critical role during the second world war helping the Allies by supplying fuel from England under the Channel to France.

Callenders supplied cables for warplanes, ships and tanks. The company also developed a buoyancy cable to deflect magnetic mines. Callender-Hamilton bridges were erected over bomb craters and used to replace destroyed bridges.

Callenders and British Insulated Cables merged in 1945.

The newly-formed group could produce almost every type of cable. The factory at Prescot also produced accessories, fittings and cable jointing; there were foundries and machine shops, pattern-makers, blacksmiths, joiners' shops and research laboratories.

A new name, British Insulated Callenders Cables Ltd, shortened to BICC, became known worldwide. With assets exceeding £140 million and trading in over 100 countries it had more than 48,000 employees. Most were concerned with the manufacture and installation of materials and equipment for the generation and distribution of electricity. Many were directly concerned with railway electrification.

In 1947 a BICC subsidiary, the British Insulated Callenders Construction Company, was relocated to Kirkby.

Above: *A staff dance in Blackpool, 1953.* **Right:** *One of the last remaining BIW Lamps, produced circa 1900.*
Inset: *A close-up of the base of the lamp with its inscription which reads British Insulated Wire Co Ltd Prescot.*

Balfour Beatty was founded in 1909 by George Balfour, a mechanical and electrical engineer, and Andrew Beatty, a chartered accountant.

The company's first contract was for a new tramway system in Dunfermline in Fife. Worth £141,450, it involved laying new track and lighting cables and installing additional generating plant at the power house. The company subsequently moved into civil engineering.

Balfour Beatty has been responsible for both design, supply and installation of many major overhead rail and tramway projects in the UK and overseas, including the Channel Tunnel.

In 1997 Balfour Beatty Rail Projects Ltd was formed to bring various rail organisations and disciplines within Balfour Beatty together to carry out multi-disciplinary

projects worldwide. The design element of the business remained in Liverpool and was involved in the major project to upgrade the West Coast main line railway.

Today the site of the original Prescot works is now Cables Retail Park, retaining in its name a memory for those who spent their lives working in the cable industry.

Morris Jones - Covering the City

The firm of Morris Jones & Son, Carpet Specialists, is well known in Liverpool. Its story began around 1885 when B Hembry & Company, Linoleum and Oilcloth Merchants of London, open a Liverpool branch in North John Street.

A Mr Over came from London as manager and took on a Mr Morris Jones. Ten years later Morris married Mr Over's daughter, Mary Ann. In the following year Over died, leaving Mary Ann a small amount of money owed to him by Hembrys. The firm, in financial trouble, paid her not in money but with stock. It was with this small amount of stock that Morris and Mary Ann Jones set up in business in 1897.

Morris took part of a small shop in Old Hall Street. The range of good he offered sounds impressive: 'Table baizes, Blinds, Stair Linoleums, Oilcloth, Rugs and Carpets.' In reality he took no more than £200 in his first year's turnover. During those early years he frequently handed over his watch to the pawnbroker in order to provide for his family.
Gradually however, business began to improve. Morris

moved to bigger premises at 59 Tithebarn Street. Then, in 1906 he moved to Dale Street. He was acquiring a good reputation: the next year he was awarded the flooring work in the new Liverpool Cotton Association Building in Old Hall Street.

In 1913 the business was nearly sunk when Morris' brother, who owned a tailoring business in Islington, fled to New Zealand leaving a string of debts. Morris, unwisely, had agreed to act as guarantor. Not having enough to pay off the debts, he reached an accommodation allowing him to continue trading while the money was repaid: it took him two years.

In 1914 Morris moved into basement premises in Covent Garden. Meanwhile, in 1911, Morris's 14 year old son, Morris William Jones, had joined the business. Serving in the Army during the first world war, Morris William was injured and gassed. In 1919 he was invalided home with a 90 percent disability pension. A determined young man, he returned to his father's business and never missed a day's work until he retired in 1967.

After Morris senior died in 1932, Morris William faced the Depression years alone, at one stage surviving on a profit margin of little more than 6 percent before expenses and working very long hours.

In the years before the second world war most of the work came from Local Authority tenders, some shipping and shop fitting. Each of the first 80 shops opened by the Sayers Bakery chain was fitted with linoleum by Morris Jones. By 1939 Morris was employing six fitters, but soon they were all called up in the Armed Services, leaving just Morris and an elderly handyman. With a wife and three young sons to support, Morris ran the business single-handed throughout the war.

After the war, married couples were issued with dockets entitling them to 20 square yards of linoleum. However, there was no stock to honour them. This was the situation that Morris Edward Jones found when he left school. In the family business his father demanded his own meticulous standards from his son and got them. When Morris William retired in 1967 the foundations of skill and reliability on which the firm was built continued into the next generation.

Morris's brother, Ron, who joined him in 1967, is now Chairman of the Company, although both brothers have retired from the day-to-day running of the business.

Today the Company is in the hands of the next generation: Managing Director, Chris Hughes, who has been with the firm for over twenty years, heads up the contract flooring operation from their Liverpool premises at 16 Cook Street, while Morris's son, Brian, is Director of retail sales based in Greasby, Wirral. With its team of first-class, loyal staff, the Company continues to thrive.

Morris Jones & Son has had to diversify with its product portfolio in recent years to meet today's more discerning customers and now offer Wood, Cork, Rubber, Decorative Vinyl tiles, Laminate and Natural Flooring as well as traditional Axminster and Wilton patterned and plain carpeting to its retail clients.

Morris Jones & Son Contracts division has carried out installations in all of Liverpool's most famous landmarks and continues to grow from strength to strength with its quality product knowledge and service.

By far the oldest established carpet business on Merseyside, Morris Jones & Son look set for another century of progress, and there is no doubt in Chris and Brian's minds that this is due to the personal service and emphasis on quality that are typical of the family tradition. As Chris and Brian say "We are not big by today's standards but we do like to think we are the best".

Facing page: An early 20th century picture of Tower Building where Morris Jones & Son were located before moving to Cook Street in 2003, the picture shows a very different view of Liverpool to that which is familiar today. **Right:** *One of only two buildings by the Liverpool architect, Peter Ellis, 16 Cook Street. Built two years after Oriel Chambers, it shows a development of his style. The front elevation consist of three bays with a Venetian headed window, but as with Oriel Chambers, it is once again at the rear of building that contains the most remarkable feature. A glazed cast iron spiral staircase dominates the narrow courtyard. The spiral has no central support, but appears to be cantilevered from each floor. It has been speculated that the influence of this can be seen in the early skyscrapers in Chicago where the American architect John Root who, having been sent to abroad to avoid the Civil War, was in Liverpool at the time that Cook Street was being built. Some of his work shows close influences of Peter Ellis. After Cook Street, the only recorded work by Ellis is as a civil engineer.*

Liverpool College - Learning for life

The City of Liverpool is buzzing with renewed self-confidence and vitality. The towering cranes of the developers dominate the skyline, a tell-tale sign of a city on the way up. And like the city Liverpool College too is boldly striding forward.

Liverpool College is an Independent Day School for boys and girls between the ages of three and eighteen.

Taught by first-class teachers pupils achieve first-class results, and they move confidently on to university and into the wider world as talented, rounded individuals. At the heart of an important conservation area, on the edge of Sefton Park, the fine 26-acre campus provides the ideal setting in which to offer students the continuity of education upon which the school's reputation rests.

Founded in 1840, the original school was in Shaw Street where the buildings were designed by Harvey Lonsdale Elmes, the architect of the famous St George's Hall. These buildings later became Liverpool Collegiate, and the College moved to new premises late in the 19th century, before making a final move before the last war to its present site at Mossley Hill.

The school comprises a mixture of large Victorian merchants' houses and purpose-built facilities including a Chapel and Swimming Pool. There is also an award winning Design and Technology Centre, a large Sports Hall, Information and Communication Technology suites and completely refurbished Science Laboratories.

The School provides a continuous course of education for pupils in three separate departments. Godwyn House (the Infant School and Nursery) caters for about 200 pupils up to the age of seven, while Mossley Vale (the Junior School) has a further 200 pupils from seven to eleven. The Upper School of about 600 takes pupils from eleven to eighteen.

The Governors offer a range of Scholarships for academically gifted pupils and for Music, Art, Drama and Sport.

Pupils follow a broad curriculum to GCSE and thereafter choose three or four subjects from a choice of about

Top: *The College buildings and grounds in the 1930s. Queens Drive crosses the foreground of the picture.*
Left: *Lord Derby inspecting the cadet Officers Training Corps (OTC) on the 28th November 1924.*

site, retaining the playing fields and outstanding sports amenities to the east. There will be new accommodation for the Pre-prep and Nursery, a refurbishment and extension of the Prep School, and a complete re-build for the Upper School. The plan envisages a new Dining Hall and Performing Arts Centre, and – vital for pupil safety – a one-way route through the College with secure drop-off points and dedicated parking areas.

It is intended to move ahead quickly with this ambitious and comprehensive development plan, beginning with an exciting Learning and Resources Centre, to include Sixth Form facilities, a library and IT areas, conference, seminar and interview rooms. The Liverpool College Study Centre will take advantage of all the latest developments in education and technology and will offer a clear statement of its determined intent to give students the head-start they deserve.

The Principal Brian Christian believes that a 21st Century education should prepare young people to take their place in a society where there are very few certainties and even fewer boundaries. Who knows where the College's 14 year olds will be when they are 30? The young girl sitting her SATS this summer might well find herself in the Chicago office of some major multi-national; the boy next to her could turn out to be a globe-trotting medic in the middle of a Third World crisis.

twenty for A Level study; nearly all go on to university after the Sixth Form and on average, five or six pupils gain entry to Oxford or Cambridge each year.

All pupils participate in a wide range of sporting and other activities including the Duke of Edinburgh Award Scheme, Combined Cadet Force, Community Service, Choirs, Bands, Orchestras and many Clubs and Societies.

Former pupils include Noel Chavasse, VC and Bar, Sir Rex Harrison, Derek Guyler, Lord Hunt of Wirral, the Bishop of Wakefield, Sir Simon Rattle, Richard Stilgoe, Elton Welsby, Olympic athlete Curtis Robb and Ken Cranston, a former England Cricket Captain.

Over the next few years it is intended to concentrate the teaching and learning facilities on the western side of the

Like Liverpool itself the College is determinedly inclusive, building upon the secure foundation of its Christian principles but welcoming & enjoying the multi-faith community so representative of a modern, vibrant city.

Top: One of the Victorian houses on the school campus now used for Art and Design, Music and Music.
Above: A College boarder in the late 1940s wearing the School House blazer and cap badges. *Right:* Founders Day at Liverpool Cathedral, 2005

Porters - A century of flying the flag for Liverpool

When footballing legend George Best died in 2005 there was only one firm in England deserving of the honour of making his specially commissioned Manchester United coffin drape: Porters of Liverpool now in its centenary year.

Over its history Porters, based at King's Dock Mill, Tabley Street has supplied its products on many important occasions. The firm made the curtains for the entrance of the opening of the Mersey Tunnel in 1934 - though only after staff worked through the night adding Liver Birds to the original design! Later it supplied flags for the Queen's Coronation and Silver Jubilee. In 1965 Porters made the coffin drape for Sir Winston Churchill's funeral. Ranulph Fiennes came to Porters in 1982 to buy a flag for his expedition to the North Pole and in 1986 an RAF pilot aboard the space shuttle Challenger carried a Porters flag with him. Most notably in 1999 an historic Porters flag used by Captain Scott in 1912 to set into the snow at the South Pole was sold at auction for £25,300.

Herbert Gordon Porter set up the world famous flag-making firm Porter Brothers Ltd of Liverpool during the years before the outbreak of the first world war. Before setting up his own business the company founder gathered experience working for the shipping merchants in Liverpool. Herbert noticed that the shipping merchants were always being asked for flags. At that time there were no flag makers in the city and the merchants found it very difficult to meet their customers' demands. Herbert saw a gap in the market and decided to it by setting up a flag making business of his own.

Launching his fledgling venture on the Dock Road Herbert employed a couple of machinists to help with production. He must have been a fair employer as the machinists both worked for Porters for over fifty years! In the early days of the business the flags were sold to the shipping companies in the port. This trade was complemented by another side to the business run by

Above: *Porters pattern cutting room in the 1950s.*

Robert's son, Michael Gordon Porter now took over the running of the firm as its Managing Director. Robert Porter died in 2003: today, following a management buy-out in 2005, Michael Porter remains with the company as a consultant whilst the current Managing Director is Barry Clare, previously the firm's Company Director/Secretary.

Today, after a century in business, Porters employs some 25 people; many of its flags are manufactured for the British armed forces and for advertising purposes. Although it still maintains the tradition of making flags by hand, Porters has also adopted the latest technology and can supply digitally printed flags for displays and exhibitions. The company also supplies high quality cleaning cloths for Airbus and a wide range of packaging materials. Porters is still flying the flag of success for Liverpool.

Herbert's brother Harry who was in charge of supplying cleaning and wiping rags to the ships' merchants.

The business had developed to such an extent by the 1920s that it was necessary to move to new premises further along the Old Dock road. From there as well as the production of flags, cotton waste was delivered for engine cleaning: rags and off-cuts bought from the Lancashire factories were cleaned using the laundry down the road. Porters became a limited company in 1921.

The company employed 20 to 30 staff by the 1930s. With their help and that of agents across the world and the Crown Agents in London, it began to build up a valuable export business supplying governments across the world.

The second world war brought with it changes to the company. Porters had been making Nazi flags for the Germans: the onset of war inevitably saw this order being cancelled. But despite that set back work was far from scarce. Throughout hostilities Porters conducted a lot of work for the MoD and even made flags for the D-day landings.

By the 1950s Porters had developed even further, by now employing up to 80 staff. When Herbert took semi-retirement in the 1960s he passed on a flourishing concern on to his son Robert Gordon Porter.

In 1973, founder, Herbert Porter died. However under his son's leadership the firm continued to thrive.

Robert Porter took semi-retirement in 1994, though continued to work part time.

Above: *Porters trucks loading up, 1950s.*
Below: *The largest flag ever made at the time of the Queen's visit to Australia in 1954.*

There's no business like Hayes & Finch

Liverpool's Hayes & Finch Ltd is truly unique. Today the firm employs some 80 people in its Liverpool head office and factory, and a further 26 in offices in London, Scotland, Birmingham, Yorkshire, and Ireland as well as sales staff in Philadelphia and California, USA.

The only wick manufacturer in Britain, the company boasts manufacturing some 1,500 different wick product lines.

The firm employs a selection of highly skilled workers including silversmiths, vestment makers, church cabinet makers and candle makers: customers are primarily Britain's 24,000 members of the clergy.

But how did such an unusual company come into being?

In 1882, William Hayes and James Finch set up business in Old Leeds Street, Liverpool as candle manufacturers and suppliers of other church requirements. Family members still work in the business - including Chairman Simon Finch, and Director Charles Finch, both great grandsons of the founder.

The beginnings were on a small scale, with local deliveries being made by hand carts, and outlying

Top left: *Founder, James Finch.*
Below: *Company premises 1905, Vernon Street, Liverpool.*

areas of the city and Birkenhead supplied using hired horse-drawn wagons.

With dedication and hard work the small business prospered. In 1890s the company moved premises to a purpose built factory in Vernon Street, Liverpool, opened an additional candle making factory in Dublin and further sales offices in London and Glasgow.

In 1905 Hayes & Finch became a limited company run by Mr Hayes and Mr Thomas Finch, son of the late Mr James Finch the original founder.

Together they expanded the business and opened sales offices in Glasgow, London and Manchester, a wax bleaching works in Crosby and a candle factory in Dublin. In 1923 Mr Hayes died, leaving Thomas Finch the sole proprietor of the company.

The ensuing years were a great challenge to Thomas Finch, not only had he to steer the company through its early teething troubles, but he also had to repay the original share of the capital to the widow of William Hayes

Thomas James Finch, the son of the co-founder, fathered six sons who in turn followed him into the business. Through him they learned the most important lesson concerning the conduct of a business, namely, to ensure that the customer should always receive every possible courtesy and attention, and be offered true value for money.

The advent of the second world war forced the closure of the Dublin factory due to the impossibility of

Above: Early wine production at Hayes & Finch.
Right: An example of the beautiful craftsmanship of a crucifix produced by Hayes and Finch

obtaining raw materials for candle making.

During this period the company virtually went into mothballs. All the sons and other able-bodied staff either volunteered or were conscripted into the armed services. By the grace of God, all returned safely. Miraculously, the factory in Vernon Street was unscathed by the repeated bombing attacks upon the city, although buildings on all sides of the factory were either destroyed or severely damaged.

The post war period in the history of the company saw branches and depots being established in Birmingham, Newcastle and Huddersfield, the latter replacing the Manchester branch. At the same time, a new branch in Dublin was opened to continue the service given prior to the war but the Dublin candle factory remained closed.

In 1969 the company moved out of the Vernon Street factory and into a modern purpose-built factory on Aintree Industrial Estate. Modern candle-making machinery and ancillary equipment was installed to enable the company to offer the best quality in candles. The move to Aintree also saw the development of other in-house production units: Wine Cellar, Metal Shop, Plating Shop, Wick Manufacture, Vestment Department and a 'state-of-the-art' Furniture Factory.

More recently, Hayes & Finch has continued to expand with the company's first sales office in the USA being opened in January 2005 in Exton, Pennsylvania. May 2006 saw further growth, with a second American branch to the east of San Francisco, California.

Every sacristy and furnishing requirement is now available directly from Hayes & Finch and delivered to

clients' doors by the firm's own transport fleet. Today after more than 120 years in business, Hayes and Finch Ltd remains committed to its original objective of providing the very best of service and products to all its valued customers.

There really is no business like Hayes & Finch.

Collinge Hairdressing- A cut above the rest

From Bishops to pop stars and from captains of industry to footballers and their wives, all are familiar figures to the Andrew Collinge hairdressing chain based throughout the North West

For over 50 years the winning Collinge formula has not changed: hairdressing of the highest standard, together with a friendly and professional service in stylish surroundings.

The Andrew Collinge Academy is a Liverpool institution. Over 200 trainees pass through the Academy each year.

Today Andrew Collinge Salon Solutions is one of the UK's most successful product ranges sold nationally through supermarkets and high street chemists. The products are available in Australia, New Zealand and the Far East. There is also a popular range of electrical haircare appliances.

A new flagship salon recently opened at 45 Castle Street, Liverpool; other prestigious salons include Manchester city centre and Selfridges & Co, Trafford Centre.

Peter Collinge opened his first salon in 1953. In 1942 Peter started out as an apprentice at a salon in Richmond Street, called Symonds, a ladies' hairdressers and wig maker.

In 1945 Peter left Symonds and for two years worked as a hairdresser on the troop ship HMS Mauritania. In 1947 Peter spent a year working with Cunard on ships based out of Southampton and New York.

Peter returned to Liverpool in 1948 and worked with his father. It was during 1950 that Peter started entering

Above: Founder, Peter Collinge.
Below: Hazel Collinge on reception at Peter Collinge Hairdressing, Hepworth Chambers, circa 1958.

hairdressing competitions with his future wife, Hazel, as his model. Between 1951 and 1953 Peter won many awards, achieving 1st place seven times.

Peter Collinge opened his own salon in June 1953 with just three employees: one hairdresser and two apprentices offering ladies a haircut for just 10/6.

That first salon was located in Church Street above Hepworth Chambers. Within a couple of years the staff grew from four to twenty.

Whilst Peter dealt with clients his wife, Hazel, worked on reception. Hazel became involved with salon design as more salons opened.

By the late 1960s there was a chain of Peter Collinge salons throughout Merseyside, and a move was made to the St Johns Centre. Other salons were opened on Wirral and Ormskirk.

In the mid-1970s the company became involved in training as part of the Government policy to train young people to learn skills in a more structured way.

In 1974 Peter Collinge was elected President of the Fellowship for British Hairdressing. That same year Andrew Collinge, Peter's son, started his career with the company.

Andrew's clientele would eventually include Peter and Zara Phillips and the Duke and Duchess of Westminster. Andrew was also invited by Sophie the Countess of Wessex to style her hair for her wedding to Prince Edward.

After working in London Andrew's sister Sarah joined the company in 1985. She now heads the training division which was recently awarded 'Beacon Status' by the Government.

Andrew Collinge went on to become President of the Fellowship for British Hairdressing in the 1990s. In 1993 he was the first English hairdresser outside of London to win the prestigious British Hairdresser of the Year award: he won the award again in 1997. In 2000 Andrew was voted International Hairdresser of the Year by the world's Hairdressing press.

In 1998 Andrew and his make-up artist wife Liz were invited to appear on the TV show 'This Morning'. They went on to weave their makeover magic for over nine years.

Peter Collinge received a Lifetime Achievement Award from the Fellowship for British Hairdressing. Andrew Collinge was recently the first recipient for the Lifetime Achievement Award presented by the Guild of Hairdressers. In 2005 Andrew received an Honorary Fellowship from Liverpool John Moores University in recognition of his contribution to Business.

Although today Peter and Hazel Collinge are not directly involved with the day to day running of the business, Peter is Company Chairman. Andrew Collinge is Managing Director, Sarah Collinge is Training Director and Liz Collinge is a Director, with her role particularly involved with the beauty and make-up departments.

A company as large and diverse as Andrew Collinge Hairdressing requires many loyal and talented people, from Administration staff to Artistic Directors. There is also an Artistic Team which represent the company on photo shoots, seminars and fashion shows. Today the once small company employs a team of over 200.

Above: *A Peter Collinge price list from the 1950s.*
Below: *Andrew Collinge Hair & Beauty Flagship Salon, Castle Street.* **Inset:** *Award-winning Hairdresser and Managing Director Andrew Collinge.*

Jacob's Bakery - A cracker of a firm

Jacob's came to Aintree in 1910 but its history began in 1841 when a small-time baker, Thomas Huntley, struck a business deal with his cousin George Palmer. The two of them founded a factory in 1846 when George invented Europe's first modern biscuit-making machine.

Meanwhile, in 1850, W.B. Jacob went into partnership with his brother Robert to manufacture 'fancy biscuits'. In 1851 they opened a factory in Dublin. The famous Cream Cracker was introduced in 1885.

As limited space round the Dublin factory precluded extension, the building of the Aintree factory was begun.

The factory stood practically in open country. It was completed in 1914. During the First World War 262 employees enlisted, 26 being killed in action and many more being wounded. Twenty men were taken prisoners of

war and, in each case the firm paid for the food parcels which were sent out by the POW organisations. With one exception all the founders' grandsons joined the Army. Jacob's contributed a Leyland lorry to the British Red Cross Society. Many employees enlisted for work in their own time in the RAMC helping when hospital ships brought wounded servicemen home.

Both the Dublin and Aintree factories produced 'Ration' biscuits for the forces. Immediately after the war the Club biscuit was launched.

In 1921 Associated Biscuits was formed through the merger of Peek Frean and Huntley & Palmer. The establishment of the Irish Free State in 1922 made it advisable to create a separate Jacob's company in England

Above: Early advertising for Jacob's Cream Crackers.
Below: The Jacob's & Co Aintree Biscuit Factory in the late 1920s.

Jacob's concentrated on fewer lines and greater standardisation. In the fifties a large expansion programme was carried out costing £3 1/2 million. Modern ovens were installed, together with laminators specially adapted for Cream Cracker production, to ensure a continuous sheet of high quality dough being fed to all ovens. Further buildings were put up and an electronically controlled flour silo was completed.

Jacob's has always looked after the welfare of its employees. In 1957 an existing building became a modern medical centre with doctors, nurses, dentists and chiropodists in attendance. After the war a comprehensive contributory pension scheme was set up and the Board erected a new pavilion and dressing rooms for the employees' sports' club. There are football teams, male and female hockey teams, netball and cricket. Tennis courts and a bowling green were provided. In 1958 the company opened a new employees' canteen costing £90,000

In 1962 the Domino and Golf biscuits were launched followed, in 1968, by the Orange biscuit, all three of which were incorporated into the Club range.

In 2004 Jacob's became part of United Biscuits.

Why the big fuss over Cream Crackers? Jacob's attribute it to the secret and unique recipe with its baking process that spans more than 14 hours!

Above: Cream Cracker being packaged for export.
Below: Biscuit dough being conveyed to the oven, circa 1960.

with control over the factory at Aintree and sales in Great Britain. When the Liverpool company formed land and buildings were valued at £135,000 and factory machinery at £75,000. Now, in addition to rail depots in Liverpool, Manchester and London, new ones were set up in Birmingham, Norwich, Southampton, Plymouth, Bristol, Cardiff and, later, Newcastle. Jacob's own vans operating from these points offered grocers a prompt delivery service.

Albert Jacob, after entering Parliament, left the guidance of these changes to his sons, Cedric and Maitland. Under them the site continued to expand, a third block being added in the late twenties and in 1934 an air-conditioned building to handle chocolate and sandwich biscuits. Another brand to become synonymous with the Aintree factory, Twiglets, was launched in 1932 by Peek Frean, and became a Jacob's brand following its merger with Associated Biscuits. Originally the savoury snack was a Christmas treat but its popularity soon ensured year round sales.

Cedric died in 1937. His son Neil Jacob took his place, becoming production director from 1947.

The second world war meant more Army biscuits but it was still possible to keep up a restricted production for civilian consumption. The factory offered temporary accommodation to government departments, Civil Defence units and bombed out industries. Actual damage suffered at Aintree was mainly confined to broken windows though the company's other depots were not so lucky. The post-war era brought more changes. Trade was hedged round with the rationing of ingredients and price controls.

Royal & SunAlliance - A premium service

Today Royal & SunAlliance is one of the world's leading multinational quoted insurance groups, writing business in 130 countries and with major operations in the United Kingdom, Scandinavia, Canada, Ireland, the Middle East and Latin America. Focussing on general insurance it has around 27,000 staff and, in 2004, its net written premiums were £5.2 billion. With almost 300 years of history behind it the company is one of the oldest insurance companies in the word.

The modern company was created by a merger in the 1990s of two of Britain's premier insurance companies: SunAlliance, and Liverpool's Royal Insurance Company.

Fire was the reason that the Royal Insurance Company was founded. Liverpool's docks and warehouses were considered to be more vulnerable to fire than others in industrial Britain. The perceived higher risk meant that the London insurance companies wanted to charge a higher premium for any Liverpool company wanting to insure against fire damage.

Following the 'Formby Street Area' fire of 1842 valuable buildings were lost at a cost of £1 million (more than £150 million today) and causing the London insurance companies to raise their premiums. Liverpool merchants were outraged at their demands, and on 11th March 1845 a

group of prominent local merchants and businessmen formed a 'Joint Stock Fire and Life Association' named Royal.

By the second half of the 19th century Liverpool was challenging London for the status of Britain's premier port. The Royal took full advantage of Liverpool's growing prosperity and made a profit in each of its first ten years.

An important milestone for the Royal was passed in 1888 when the income from fire premiums exceeded £1 million - 'the first time that any fire insurance company has ever obtained £1,000,000 sterling from fire revenue without having amalgamated with some company'.

At the end of its first fifty years the Royal was the largest fire insurer in the world, and contributed to extending the influence of British insurance across the globe.

During the next fifty years or so the company's claim-paying reputation resulted in increasing levels of new business. Despite difficult financial years in the 1920s the Royal maintained an even keel and was even able to weather the Great Depression of the early 1930s. The Royal came out of the second world war in a healthy position with new record premiums of £17.6 million for its fire, accident and marine lines, and a steady set of trading results for its overseas business.

Increasing prosperity in the 1950s and 1960s was matched by an expansion of the insurance business to cover all the public's new possessions. Difficulty in profiting from motor insurance business led to spectacular company collapses in the late 1960s and early 1970s, and the spiralling inflation of the period turned the Royal's £12.4 million UK underwriting profit of 1972 into a £5.1 million loss in 1973.

But the Royal benefited from the recession of the 1980s, with high interest rates bringing higher investment income, and a falling pound boosting overseas earnings.

Some difficult times however, still lay ahead. It was obvious that growth in the low inflation environment of the 1990s could only be sustained by sensible selective underwriting, since return on investments would be lower and could no longer be counted on to balance reduced profits from underwriting.

In 1996 The Royal merged with Sun Alliance, a company with history traceable back to 1710. The merger created Royal & SunAlliance. Today Royal & SunAlliance manages total investments of over £57 billion for over four million customers.

Within the UK Royal & SunAlliance is the second largest commercial lines insurer, covering the insurance and risk management needs of a significant number of FTSE 100 companies. It has full multi-distribution capability, writing business through brokers and corporate partners, direct and on-line. The company is also one of the UK's top three personal motor and household insurers.

The company still has roots in Liverpool with its office at New Hall Place in Old Hall Street housing 2,000 employees. From its humble beginnings Royal & SunAlliance now has a truly global presence operating worldwide.

Had those London insurers known in 1845 what remarkable seeds they were unwittingly sowing in Liverpool they would surely have had second thoughts about raising their premiums!

Top left: The Royal's fire mark which would identify buildings insured by the company and ensure that any fire would be extinguished by the Royal's own fire brigade.
Left: Many sailors from many parts of the world would know immediately where they were if they saw these three monolithic buildings on the shore. They would recognise the 'geese', the liver birds, or more correctly the cormorants roped to their perches, silhouetted against Liverpool's skyline. Below: The Royal & SunAlliance Old Hall Street office block, one of the largest in Europe.

Silverbeck Rymer - The law in safe hands

As a specialist litigation practice the Liverpool-based firm of solicitors, Silverbeck Rymer, offers expertise in Claimant, Defendant and Fraud services throughout the entire claims process. Technical insight and superior customer service has been the foundation of Silverbeck Rymer's success, which today has an annual turnover of more than £16 million.

Throughout Silverbeck Rymer's history, a variety of practice areas have been offered including criminal law, conveyancing, employment law and non-motor litigation. With offices at Liverpool (HQ) and in Chelmsford the firm now focuses on civil litigation and claims handling services to the insurance and broker market. The firm currently employs over 240 staff.

Silverbeck Rymer was established in 1946 by Nathan Silverbeck.

Nathan established himself in premises above Rigby's pub in Dale Street as a general legal practice with a strong bias towards domestic conveyancing. The firm soon began to flourish, and in 1949 Sidney Brayde joined the practice. At that time the practice had just one legal desk and two typists. Most of the work was

Top left: *Senior Partner Jim Rymer.*
Below: *A view of Dale Street at the time Nathan Silverbeck established the firm.*

still in the domestic and commercial property fields, however a small amount of work was matrimonial, criminal, insurance and general.

In 1959 the practice began to attract a larger volume of defendant insurance and other litigation work. That change was driven by a need to make up for the increasingly less remunerative domestic and conveyancing work.

Nathan Silverbeck retired in 1978. Meanwhile the firm continued to thrive, and its litigation department to grow. In 1979, to cope with the increasing workload, the firm took on another partner, Jim Rymer.

Jim had originally joined the practice as a Junior Clerk, and after qualifying was sent to take charge of newly opened branch in Bootle. It was in Bootle that Jim began to follow his own particular legal star, displaying his expertise and enthusiasm in Civil Litigation.

In the 1980s the firm began its period of rapid growth. By 1993 the firm had outgrown its city centre offices and moved to the Grade II listed Heywoods Building in Brunswick Street. Silverbeck Rymer continued its expansion by opening an office in Chelmsford in 1997.

The Claimant arm of the business was extended in 2002 with the introduction of a specialist Catastrophic Injury Unit, specialising in brain and spinal injury work. That same year the firm also established an in-house Call Centre which is now staffed by over 12 advisors.

Silverbeck Rymer identified the need for a specialised approach to handling motorcycle claims and created a dedicated department in November 2004.

The biggest development for the firm over the past decade came in 2005 when the firm moved from its City Centre location in Brunswick Street to a newly converted warehouse on the Brunswick dock. There is now approximately 200 staff based at the Liverpool office. As one era ended another exciting era began with the new HQ came advanced technology and a modern working environment for staff.

Through this continued investment in people and technology Silverbeck Rymer was named as the leading niche insurance-based law firm in England and Wales in 2005. The Award given by one of the industry's leading publications emphasised the firm's dedication to becoming a market leader within the insurance industry.

Working in partnership with the UK's leading Brokers and Insurers Silverbeck Rymer deliver bespoke solutions to continuously exceed their client's expectations. Technical insight and superior customer service has been the foundation of Silverbeck Rymer's success which has lead to a turnover in the order of 16 million in 2005.

Today, looking from the past to the future, strategic development is a primary focus for Jim Rymer and the Silverbeck Rymer Board of Directors.

Above: Sidney Brayde.
Below: The converted warehouse on the Brunswick Dock, home of Silverbeck Rymer since 2005.

ACKNOWLEDGMENTS

The publishers would like to thank

Liverpool Libraries and Information Services

Reflections - Black & White Photographic Archive - www.20thcenturyimages.co.uk

Andrew Mitchell

Steve Ainsworth

True North Books Ltd - Book

Memories of Accrington - 1 903204 05 4

Memories of Barnet - 1 903204 16 X

Memories of Barnsley - 1 900463 11 3

More Memories of Barnsley - 1 903 204 79 8

Golden Years of Barnsley -1 900463 87 3

Memories of Basingstoke - 1 903204 26 7

Memories of Bedford - 1 900463 83 0

More Memories of Bedford - 1 903204 33 X

Golden Years of Birmingham - 1 900463 04 0

Birmingham Memories - 1 903204 45 3

More Birmingham Memories - 1 903204 80 1

Memories of Blackburn - 1 900463 40 7

More Memories of Blackburn - 1 900463 96 2

Memories of Blackpool - 1 900463 21 0

Memories of Bolton - 1 900463 45 8

More Memories of Bolton - 1 900463 13 X

Bolton Memories - 1 903204 37 2

Memories of Bournemouth -1 900463 44 X

Memories of Bradford - 1 900463 00 8

More Memories of Bradford - 1 900463 16 4

More Memories of Bradford II - 1 900463 63 6

Bradford Memories - 1 903204 47 X

Bradford City Memories - 1 900463 57 1

Memories of Bristol - 1 900463 78 4

More Memories of Bristol - 1 903204 43 7

Memories of Bromley - 1 903204 21 6

Memories of Burnley - 1 900463 95 4

Golden Years of Burnley - 1 900463 67 9

Memories of Bury - 1 900463 90 3

More Memories of Bury - 1 903 204 78 X

Memories of Cambridge - 1 900463 88 1

Memories of Cardiff - 1 900463 14 8

More Memories of Cardiff - 1 903204 73 9

Memories of Carlisle - 1 900463 38 5

Memories of Chelmsford - 1 903204 29 1

Memories of Cheltenham - 1 903204 17 8

Memories of Chester - 1 900463 46 6

More Memories of Chester -1 903204 02 X

Chester Memories - 1 903204 83 6

Memories of Chesterfield -1 900463 61 X

More Memories of Chesterfield - 1 903204 28 3

Memories of Colchester - 1 900463 74 1

Nostalgic Coventry - 1 900463 58 X

Coventry Memories - 1 903204 38 0

Memories of Croydon - 1 900463 19 9

More Memories of Croydon - 1 903204 35 6

Golden Years of Darlington - 1 900463 72 5

Nostalgic Darlington - 1 900463 31 8

Darlington Memories - 1 903204 46 1

Memories of Derby - 1 900463 37 7

More Memories of Derby - 1 903204 20 8

Memories of Dewsbury & Batley - 1 900463 80 6

Memories of Doncaster - 1 900463 36 9

More Memories of Doncaster - 1 903204 75 5

Nostalgic Dudley - 1 900463 03 2

Golden Years of Dudley - 1 903204 60 7

Memories of Edinburgh - 1 900463 33 4

More memories of Edinburgh - 1903204 72 0

Memories of Enfield - 1 903204 14 3

Memories of Exeter - 1 900463 94 6

Memories of Glasgow - 1 900463 68 7

More Memories of Glasgow - 1 903204 44 5

Memories of Gloucester - 1 903204 04 6

Memories of Grimsby - 1 900463 97 0

More Memories of Grimsby - 1 903204 36 4

Memories of Guildford - 1 903204 22 4

Memories of Halifax - 1 900463 05 9

More Memories of Halifax - 1 900463 06 7

Golden Years of Halifax - 1 900463 62 8

Nostalgic Halifax - 1 903204 30 5

Memories of Harrogate - 1 903204 01 1

Memories of Hartlepool - 1 900463 42 3

Memories of High Wycombe - 1 900463 84 9

Memories of Huddersfield - 1 900463 15 6

More Memories of Huddersfield - 1 900463 26 1

Golden Years of Huddersfield - 1 900463 77 6

Nostalgic Huddersfield - 1 903204 19 4

Huddersfield Memories - 1903204 86 0

Huddersfield Town FC - 1 900463 51 2

Memories of Hull - 1 900463 86 5

More Memories of Hull - 1 903204 06 2

Hull Memories - 1 903204 70 4

True North Books Ltd - Book

Memories of Keighley - 1 900463 01 6

Golden Years of Keighley - 1 900463 92 X

Memories of Kingston - 1 903204 24 0

Memories of Leeds - 1 900463 75 X

More Memories of Leeds - 1 900463 12 1

Golden Years of Leeds - 1 903204 07 0

Memories of Leicester - 1 900463 08 3

Leeds Memories - 1 903204 62 3

More Memories of Leicester - 1 903204 08 9

Memories of Leigh - 1 903204 27 5

Memories of Lincoln - 1 900463 43 1

Memories of Liverpool - 1 900463 07 5

More Memories of Liverpool - 1 903204 09 7

Liverpool Memories - 1 903204 53 4

More Liverpool Memories - 1 903204 88 7

Memories of Luton - 1 900463 93 8

Memories of Macclesfield - 1 900463 28 8

Memories of Manchester - 1 900463 27 X

More Memories of Manchester - 1 903204 03 8

Manchester Memories - 1 903204 54 2

Memories of Middlesbrough - 1 900463 56 3

More Memories of Middlesbrough - 1 903204 42 9

Memories of Newbury - 1 900463 79 2

Memories of Newcastle - 1 900463 81 4

More Memories of Newcastle - 1 903204 10 0

Newcastle Memories - 1.903204 71 2

Memories of Newport - 1 900463 59 8

Memories of Northampton - 1 900463 48 2

More Memories of Northampton - 1 903204 34 8

Memories of Norwich - 1 900463 73 3

Memories of Nottingham - 1 900463 91 1

More Memories of Nottingham - 1 903204 11 9

Nottingham Memories - 1 903204 63 1

Bygone Oldham - 1 900463 25 3

Memories of Oldham - 1 900463 76 8

More Memories of Oldham - 1 903204 84 4

Memories of Oxford - 1 900463 54 7

Memories of Peterborough - 1 900463 98 9

Golden Years of Poole - 1 900463 69 5

Memories of Portsmouth - 1 900463 39 3

More Memories of Portsmouth - 1 903204 51 8

Nostalgic Preston - 1 900463 50 4

More Memories of Preston - 1 900463 17 2

Preston Memories - 1 903204 41 0

Memories of Reading - 1 900463 49 0

Memories of Rochdale - 1 900463 60 1

More Memories of Reading - 1 903204 39 9

More Memories of Rochdale - 1 900463 22 9

Memories of Romford - 1 903204 40 2

Memories of Rotherham- 1903204 77 1

Memories of St Albans - 1 903204 23 2

Memories of St Helens - 1 900463 52 0

Memories of Sheffield - 1 900463 20 2

More Memories of Sheffield - 1 900463 32 6

Golden Years of Sheffield - 1 903204 13 5

Memories of Slough - 1 900 463 29 6

Golden Years of Solihull - 1 903204 55 0

Memories of Southampton - 1 900463 34 2

More Memories of Southampton - 1 903204 49 6

Memories of Stockport - 1 900463 55 5

More Memories of Stockport - 1 903204 18 6

Stockport Memories - 1 903204 87 9

Memories of Stockton - 1 900463 41 5

Memories of Stoke-on-Trent - 1 900463 47 4

More Memories of Stoke-on-Trent - 1 903204 12 7

Memories of Stourbridge - 1903204 31 3

Memories of Sunderland - 1 900463 71 7

More Memories of Sunderland - 1 903204 48 8

Memories of Swindon - 1 903204 00 3

Memories of Uxbridge - 1 900463 64 4

Memories of Wakefield - 1 900463 65 2

More Memories of Wakefield - 1 900463 89 X

Nostalgic Walsall - 1 900463 18 0

Golden Years of Walsall - 1 903204 56 9

More Memories of Warrington - 1 900463 02 4

Warrington Memories - 1 903204 85 2

Memories of Watford - 1 900463 24 5

Golden Years of West Bromwich - 1 900463 99 7

Memories of Wigan - 1 900463 85 7

Golden Years of Wigan - 1 900463 82 2

More Memories of Wigan - 1 903204 82 8

Nostalgic Wirral - 1 903204 15 1

Wirral Memories - 1 903204 747

Memories of Woking - 1 903204 32 1

Nostalgic Wolverhampton - 1 900463 53 9

Wolverhampton Memories - 1 903204 50 X

Memories of Worcester - 1 903204 25 9

Memories of Wrexham - 1 900463 23 7

Memories of York - 1 900463 66 0

Available in the Local Interest section of all major bookshops or direct from the publishers - telephone 01422 344344